• • •

Brenda Waggoner's voice is like a thunderstorm on the parched Texas panhandle. If you are experiencing a spiritual dry spell, the refreshing rain of the second chapter alone is an oasis for the arid soul. *Fairy Tale Faith* is a gem.

—**Brennan Manning,** author of *The Wisdom of Tenderness*

• • •

We have grown up in a world of fairy-tale love and unrealistic expectations. Brenda Waggoner takes us on a journey that will help us embrace reality as we are wrapped in the truth that God loves us just as we are. This book is not just good; it's a must-read for every . . . woman who has ever struggled with happily ever after!

—**Debbie Alsdorf,** director of women's ministries, Cornerstone Fellowship, and author of *Restoring Love*

• • •

What a wonderful book! Brenda Waggoner writes with wisdom, insight, and biblical truth. This is a book that will make you free and allow you to dance. Read it and be glad!

—**Steve Brown,** author and Bible teacher on *Key Life* radio program

• • •

A treasure of tender, caring words from an authentic voice, *Fairy Tale Faith* is a book to savor, to share, to turn to again and again as one would turn to a trusted friend for counsel and encouragement. Wisely, gently, Brenda Waggoner shows us how to "become strong enough to bear reality one day at a time."

—**Jan Winebrenner,** author of *Intimate Faith*

• • •

Comfort through Christ! Brenda Waggoner has experienced it, and now she uses her God-given talents as a licensed professional counselor and author of *Fairy Tale Faith* to share that comfort with other women. You will learn that you are more than your circumstances. You are a child of God.

—**John Gillespie,** executive director of Roaring-Lambs.org

• • •

Fairy Tale Faith weaves the stories, movies, and tales you know with the stories and tales from Brenda Waggoner's rich walk with God. The result is a compelling book that takes us beyond our own disillusionment into the hope of an everlasting Love.

—**Jan Meyers,** licensed professional counselor and
author of *The Allure of Hope: God's Pursuit of a Woman's Heart*

• • •

Reading *Fairy Tale Faith* is like basking in the gentle wisdom of a trusted friend. Brenda Waggoner captures the heart of women: our fierce hunger for the life of our dreams; our deep disappointment when relationships, careers, and bodies fall short of those dreams; and our daily struggle to experience something meaningful with God. *Fairy Tale Faith* reminds us of this simple truth: Being in relationship with God and being present with life as it really is are one and the same.

—**Ruth McGinnis,** musician, motivational speaker,
and author of *Breathing Freely*

• • •

Like a soothing cup of hot chocolate on a frosty morning, Brenda warms our shriveled souls and deadened hearts with life-savoring truth. She reminds us that God zealously loves us in spite of our sin and that he is always with us even if we don't see him, sense him, or understand him. I enthusiastically recommend *Fairy Tale Faith* for those of us who from time to time have lost our way searching for "happily ever after."

—**Leslie Vernick,** Christian counselor, speaker,
and author of *How to Act Right When Your Spouse Acts Wrong*

• • •

I have known Brenda for years, and it is so encouraging to see how God works through her to connect with women out of her own experience. God's healing work in Brenda—from disillusionment and pain to hope and vulnerability—gives her understanding and credibility beyond the norm. My friend doesn't offer a pointing finger but rather a helping hand out of the pit she knew all too well.

—**Gene Getz,** pastor and author of *The Measure of a Church*

BRENDA WAGGONER

Fairy Tale Faith

Living in the meantime when you expected happily ever after

TYNDALE HOUSE PUBLISHERS, INC.
WHEATON, ILLINOIS

Visit Tyndale's exciting Web site at www.tyndale.com

Fairy Tale Faith: Living in the Meantime When You Expected Happily Ever After

Copyright © 2003 by Brenda Waggoner. All rights reserved.

Cover illustration copyright © 2002 by donna Kae Nelson. All rights reserved.

Author photograph copyright © 2002 by Joy Allen. All rights reserved.

Designed by Julie Chen

Edited by Susan Taylor

Published in association with the literary agency of Alive Communications, Inc., 7680 Goddard Street, Suite 200, Colorado Springs, CO 80920.

The poem on page 134 is copyrighted 1982 by Brenda Waggoner. All rights reserved.

The poem on page 157 is copyrighted 1993 by Brenda Waggoner. All rights reserved.

Some of the anecdotal illustrations in this book are true to life and are included with the permission of the persons involved. All other stories are composites of real situations with names, places, and details changed to protect confidentiality.

Unless otherwise indicated, all Scripture quotations are taken from the *Holy Bible,* New International Version®. NIV®. Copyright © 1973, 1978, 1984 by International Bible Society. Used by permission of Zondervan Publishing House. All rights reserved.

Scripture quotations marked "NKJV" are taken from the New King James Version. Copyright © 1979, 1980, 1982, 1991 by Thomas Nelson, Inc. Used by permission. All rights reserved.

Scripture quotations marked NLT are taken from the *Holy Bible,* New Living Translation, copyright © 1996. Used by permission of Tyndale House Publishers, Inc., Wheaton, Illinois 60189. All rights reserved.

Scripture quotations marked TLB are taken from *The Living Bible,* copyright © 1971. Used by permission of Tyndale House Publishers, Inc., Wheaton, Illinois 60189. All rights reserved.

Some Scripture quotations taken from *THE MESSAGE.* Copyright © by Eugene H. Peterson, 1993, 1994, 1995. Used by permission of NavPress Publishing Group.

Library of Congress Cataloging-in-Publication Data

Waggoner, Brenda
  Fairy tale faith : living in the meantime when you expected happily ever after / Brenda Waggoner.
    p. cm.
Includes bibliographical references.
  ISBN 0-8423-7113-3 (hc)
  1. Christian women—Religious life. I. Title.
BV4527 .W28 2003
248.8'43—dc21   2002154614

Printed in the United States of America

09 08 07 06 05 04 03
7   6   5   4   3   2   1

With love to Mother and Dad

Then let us agree on this: There is divine union, and there is a way to it. The way has a beginning, a progress, and a point of arrival. Furthermore, the closer you come to the consummation, the more you put aside the things that helped you get started. Of course, there is also a middle, for you cannot go from a beginning to an end without there being an intermediate space. But if the end is good and holy and necessary, and the entrance is also good, you can be sure the journey between those two points is also good!

—Madame Jeanne Guyon
Experiencing the Depths of Jesus Christ

contents

ACKNOWLEDGMENTS   XI
INTRODUCTION   XIII

1. LIVING IN THE MEANTIME   1
   When Faith Feels like a Fairy Tale

2. RECOGNIZING THE TRUE FACE OF THE KING   17
   Understanding How You Relate to God

3. DREAMING TRUTH INSTEAD OF FANTASY   35
   Learning to Stay Grounded in God

4. UNLOCKING THE DUNGEON OF SELF-HATRED   53
   Trading Self-Image for God-Image

5. RELINQUISHING THE WAND OF DENIAL   69
   Moving from Magical Thinking to Mindfulness

6. WIELDING THE SHIELD OF SELF-PROTECTION   85
   Surrendering Control in Strength, Not Weakness

7. RESISTING THE
   "OFF WITH HER HEAD" SYNDROME   103
   Nurturing the Spirit by Reclaiming the Body

8. AWAKENING TO THE KING'S KISS   121
   Reigniting Passion for God

9. ENTERING THE CASTLE OF PEACE   137
   Finding the Safe Retreat of Stillness and Solitude

10. CRYING OUT ALONE IN A DARK WOOD   155
Discovering God's Presence When He Seems Absent

11. SITTING IN THE KING'S LAP   167
Learning to Practice the Presence of God

12. LIVING IN GOD'S FAIRY TALE   183
Letting His Love Write Today's Chapter

NOTES   197
ABOUT THE AUTHOR   203

Acknowledgments

My deepest gratitude to Kathy Helmers at Alive Communications for encouragement, motivation, and catching the vision for FAIRY TALE FAITH.

Sincere thanks to Tammy Faxel, Janelle Howard, and Sue Taylor at Tyndale House for their contributions to making FAIRY TALE FAITH the book it is.

The writings of Henri Nouwen and Brennan Manning have helped liberate me from legalism, and I am forever grateful to them. I also want to acknowledge C. S. Lewis and Frederick Buechner for their deep insights into human nature, the value of fantasy at all ages, and for their encouragement to believe the unbelievable.

To those closest to my heart—Frank, Scott, Brent, Jane, Brandon—without you I would not have written this book or had the life I have grown to cherish.

When I was about eight years old, I heard Billy Graham preach the gospel to my dad from the television. I remember walking into my bedroom to sit quietly as I listened to the people singing "Just As I Am." It was the first time I recall knowing there was Someone calling to me from beyond this life, beyond this world, calling me away to be with him.

Years passed. As a young mother I heard the gospel for myself. I came to know Jesus, the One who calls me his beloved. Now I was a Christian—I had found the golden key to happiness! I set out to be an ideal wife and mother, serving in the church, teaching my children Bible stories and memorizing proverbs with them as they grew up, trying to have strong faith and raise a Christian family so we could have good lives. Life had the feel of a fairy tale, and I expected each day to ring with tones of Happily Ever After.

More years passed. Blessings and disappointments came. I succeeded and failed, laughed and cried, trusted and worried. I became confused and discouraged. *Is something wrong with me?* I wondered. My Christian life was a swirl of ecstasy and misery. But even though my life no longer felt like a fairy tale, the gospel still rang true for me.

Gradually I began to realize that for Happily Ever After, I would have to wait to get to heaven. These were the days of the Meantime. There was a tale being told all right, but it was a true story—the gospel of Jesus Christ. I was not the hero; he was. The golden key in my pocket did not control the world; he did. I began to accept and enjoy my life with

Christ more than I ever had before, to experience his presence, and to know that he *really* wants me to come to him throughout the ups and downs of life, "just as I am." The idealized dreams I once had for my life and the lives of those I love did not all come true in the way I hoped they would. But hidden blessings beyond anything I ever could have dreamed up were waiting for me to uncover them each day as I encountered Christ's presence and grace in the midst of life as it really is—not as I thought it should be.

Perhaps, like me, you expected your life to be instantly transformed into Happily Ever After the moment you came to know Christ. But now the glimmer is wearing off the edges of your idealized Christian faith, and you're becoming weary and disillusioned. Sometimes we have to clear away obstacles that block us from experiencing a meaningful, intimate relationship with God. We may be confused about his character. Perhaps our role models fell short (whose didn't?), and we ended up thinking God was like those people who failed or disappointed us. Placing our faith in Christ as our Savior is one thing. But trusting him day by day, especially if life has taught us not to trust, presents challenges. Without even realizing it, we may be subtly deceived, actually placing our confidence in our ability to have strong faith and get the results we want from our prayers instead of trusting God.

One day when we meet Jesus face-to-face, the deepest longings of our hearts will be fully fulfilled. But in the Meantime, ragged and bewildering as some days may be, our very disappointments and broken dreams can open our eyes to what Happily Ever After *really* means. As we face our deepest heartaches, walk through our pain, and look reality squarely in the eye, we find Christ right there in the midst of it, ready to embrace us no matter what has happened.

Fairy Tale Faith is written to encourage women to look beyond the unexpected turns our paths take, beyond the changes and adaptations we have to make as disappointments come, to see the invisible, absolute truth in Jesus Christ, who *never* changes. Come along with me as we explore ways of discovering intimacy with Jesus as we face the dilemmas of real everyday life.

LIVING IN THE MEANTIME

When Faith Feels like a Fairy Tale

• • •

[IN] THE FAIRY TALE OF THE GOSPEL,

THE ONE CRUCIAL DIFFERENCE FROM ALL

OTHER FAIRY TALES . . . IS THAT THE CLAIM

MADE FOR IT IS THAT IT IS TRUE, THAT IT

NOT ONLY HAPPENED ONCE UPON A TIME

BUT HAS KEPT ON HAPPENING EVER SINCE

AND IS HAPPENING STILL.

Frederick Buechner[1]

He didn't come," Buttercup sighs, when her true love doesn't rescue her as she expected. In S. Morgenstern's classic tale *The Princess Bride*, Buttercup tries to hang on to Westly's words "I will always come for you." But life leads her through seas of eel-infested waters and a fire swamp full of quicksand. Behind the scenes visible to Buttercup, Westly is fighting untold battles to save her from the wicked Prince Humperdinck, who has waged war with him over Buttercup. Occasionally Westly makes an appearance to remind her of his vow, help her fight off R.O.U.S.'s (Rodents Of Unusual Size), find her way through the bog of eternal stench.

"I will always come for you."

"How can you be sure?" Buttercup asks.

"Because it's true love."

Reassured at the sight of her Westly, Buttercup vows never to doubt again. But Humperdinck doesn't give up his relentless efforts to lure her away from her true love. At last he succeeds in deceiving Buttercup, convincing her that Westly is dead, and she agrees to marry Humperdinck. As the solemn wedding ceremony between Buttercup and Humperdinck nears its conclusion, Westly is fighting his way past castle guards, clambering past soldiers on horseback, to claim his bride before it's too late. Humperdinck hears the ruckus outside, knows Westly is on his way, and rushes the priest to conclude the ceremony, not realizing they've left out the marital vows. As Humperdinck prepares to fight Westly, he sends Buttercup to her room, where she prepares to end her life. But just before she thrusts a dagger into her chest, a wounded and bedraggled Westly limps to her bedchamber for a final standoff with Humperdinck. At last Westly has arrived just in time, coming for her as he always said he would.

The dilemmas of *The Princess Bride* are common to us as Christian women. Like Buttercup, as we slog through the quicksand and bogs of everyday life, glimpses and reminders of our True Love help us hang on to hope and believe invisible truths. When we see sure evidence of Christ's presence and blessing, we vow never to doubt again. But then Rodents Of Unusual Size attack. We can't see Jesus, and it's hard to believe he's really there. We become fearful, disillusioned, and wonder if he has forgotten us. We don't feel his love or see any outward evidence of it in our lives, and it's hard to keep believing that he does love us. Amazingly, whether we doubt him or trust him, Christ continues to fight untold battles behind the scenes on our behalf. But sometimes we lose track of what keeps the gospel ringing true.

When I became a Christian in my mid-twenties, I set out to be an ideal Christian wife and mother, to serve effectively in the church, to have strong faith and share it eagerly with people around me. But I knew nothing of the heart of God, his lavish love for us, how to be close to him, or how to recognize blessings in disguise. Over the years I began to discover God's grace through my failures and weaknesses instead of through my strengths. I discovered the love of people I cared for by being vulnerable and admitting my own human frailty instead of by chasing a mirage of perfection. I started to realize that I was surrounded by love and blessing, but it wasn't happening at all the way I had once expected it to. Instead of focusing on trusting God, I had been fixated on being an efficient Christian and getting results to my prayers.

What disappointments have invaded your life, altering your plans, shattering your dreams, taking you far away from the vision and hopes you once had for yourself and people you love when you first began your life with Christ? Perhaps you've been divorced or have longed for a child but never had one. Maybe one of your children has chosen the path of a prodigal. Perhaps a business failure drove you to bankruptcy and you've never recovered your financial stability. Maybe you have never healed from an abusive relationship that scarred you as a little girl.

To believe the truth of the gospel—that abundant life in Christ is really not about doing it all, having it all, being it all, or knowing it all but about knowing him through it all—is to practice authentic faith.

If our belief in the Christian life is limited to getting what we want for ourselves and our families—"blessing" on our own terms—we're believing in a predictable, mechanical God. That's not authentic faith. We are created for God's glory and pleasure, not our own, though often he delights in giving us what we want and ask for. But to believe throughout life's ups and downs, no matter what they are, the truth of the gospel—that Christ loved us enough to die for us; that abundant life in Christ is really not about doing it all, having it all, being it all, or knowing it all but about *knowing him through it all*—is to practice authentic faith.

I call it *Fairy Tale Faith* because it is the true story of your life as it really is—not as you thought it should be—the life that God has promised to be with you through, moment by moment. Though we relish remembering the happy endings of fairy tales, we may forget that even the heroes and heroines of such classic lore must endure heartrending trials before their lives end happily ever after. So it will be in our lives as Christians.

What have been your perplexing dilemmas, the struggles and disappointments you didn't expect to encounter once you believed the gospel? Ironically, the very trials that threaten to convince us we're not fit to be daughters of God often become his means of taking over our hearts, claiming us inch by inch. In the midst of our flawed, imperfect lives Christ's love reaches beyond our limitations and imperfections with an overcoming compassion— not erasing our pain, our past, our problems, but living with us through them, leaving us with an incurable hope and longing for what is to come.

INFORMATION OR TRANSFORMATION?

"I try to have strong faith and believe God's love and forgiveness are mine," Valerie said. "But it doesn't work. It's like trying to believe in some stupid fairy tale—I just don't get it. What is faith, really?"

After years of early sexual promiscuity and several abortions, Valerie had tried hard to believe that God loved her and had forgiven her. It sounded so simple—just read the black and white words on the pages of the Bible and walk in faith, right? As the saying goes, "God said it, I believe it, and that settles it." Valerie, now the wife of a seminary professor, had no trouble believing God had created her and blessed her from the beginning in her mother's womb. During her little-girl days she'd heard stories about King Jesus. She knew for certain that Christ would return one day to take her to live in his heavenly castle. But as Valerie squarely faced her doubts about God's love for her *today,* after she'd made so many poor choices and mistakes, she grew increasingly discouraged.

Over the course of Valerie's therapy we had discussed past wounds. She had vented anger and hurt feelings, prayed for forgiveness and healing, and claimed scriptural truths. Valerie's brain was jam-packed with Bible facts, yet she could not grasp the basic truth that she was completely forgiven and that Jesus loved her enough to die for her just as she was, mistakes and all.

Near the end of one of her counseling sessions, it occurred to me that although Valerie had accumulated a lot of information about God, it didn't appear to be making a meaningful difference in the way she lived. She knew she was *supposed* to trust God, but she had no clue about how to do it. She knew the Christian life was *supposed* to be about a relationship with Christ, yet she had no real sense of connection to him. Her faith had taken on the feel of a fantasy story because her life was not unfolding as happily or predictably as she had expected. I thought briefly of how I'd lived the first twenty years of my Christian life ignorant of the difference between accumulating information and experiencing transformation, between head knowledge about God and heartfelt awareness of him. Perhaps, like me, Valerie was longing to know God in her heart as well as in her head.

There is a difference between accumulating information and experiencing transformation, between head knowledge about God and heartfelt awareness of him.

I asked her if she'd be willing to spend five minutes each day at the end of her personal worship time just being still and quiet in the presence of God, setting her Bible and prayer list aside. If a phrase or verse from her reading had jumped out at her, she might hold it in her mind and heart, savoring its truth, or picture its reality. I hoped God might break through the barrier of the involuntary emotional isolation that had kept Valerie in bondage for so many years. She didn't know how to slow down, be still, and know God by engaging in an interactive, personal relationship with him. We'll take a deeper look at this in chapter 9.

Several weeks passed. At first Valerie said the "five minutes with God" seemed unproductive, like a total waste of time to just sit silently after she'd completed her study and prayer. But with a little encouragement she kept at it.

Then one day Valerie came into my office smiling. "One day as I was sitting still after reading through the fifth chapter of Romans," she said, "a phrase from verse 8 kept replaying in my mind: 'God showed his great love for us by sending Christ to die for us while we were still sinners' [NLT]. While we were still sinners . . . Christ died for us. . . . *While we were still sinners.* It was as if I'd never known that truth before, never seen that depth of love, to care so much for me even before I'd acknowledged my need of a Savior."

Valerie silently stared out the window as tears welled up in her eyes. "A mental picture began to form in my mind—Jesus hanging on the cross, for the love of sinners—*sinners like me.* For a few moments I felt completely loved, forgiven, and accepted. It was something I knew not only up here," she said, pointing a finger at her forehead, "but I knew it *here.*" She placed her hand over her heart. "I think maybe I'm discovering something new about faith."

Valerie had led a disciplined spiritual life for years. Yet the memories of past sins she'd confessed hundreds of times had continued to haunt her, keeping her from embracing God's grace. She had never understood what it meant to trust an invisible God when life had taught her *not* to trust people, not even herself. She hadn't known how to slow down and wait for the truths of Scripture to speak to her personally, here and now, to seep down past her intellect into her heart, engaging her in a meaningful relationship with the God who had written the Word to her.

THE ONLY TRUE FAIRY TALE

• • •

WE DON'T LOOK AT THE TROUBLES WE CAN
SEE RIGHT NOW; RATHER, WE LOOK FORWARD
TO WHAT WE HAVE NOT YET SEEN. FOR THE
TROUBLES WE SEE WILL SOON BE OVER,
BUT THE JOYS TO COME WILL LAST FOREVER.

2 Corinthians 4:18, NLT

When you look at the cold, hard facts of your life, does the evidence of God's grace seem to be stacked against you rather than for you, giving the gospel the feel of a fairy tale—a story too good to be true? Perhaps, like Valerie, you have no problem believing God created you and blessed you in your mother's womb. As a little girl you may have learned to sing "Jesus Loves Me" and even clapped your hands and danced to the joyful tune. Now that you are grown, perhaps you also know with certainty that Jesus is coming one day to take you to live with him in heaven. Once upon a Time and Happily Ever After are easy. But maybe in the Meantime your faith in God sometimes feels like something you should have outgrown by fourth grade.

In *The Uses of Enchantment,* noted child psychologist and author Bruno Bettelheim explains why children need fairy tales: "The fairy tale . . . takes these existential anxieties and dilemmas very seriously and addresses itself directly to them: the need to be loved and the fear that one is thought worthless; the love of life, and the fear of death."[2] By the time we've outgrown childhood, we all know that fairy tales are not true stories. But who among us could honestly say they no longer have doubts or fears about these same dilemmas: life, death, and especially those all-too-pervasive feelings of worthlessness?

As Christians we need to exercise the freedom to admit that we still struggle with life's complexities instead of pretend we've mastered them. Even though we may have matured in years, we will never outgrow our childlike need to trust God. Perhaps this is part of what Christ had in mind when he said, "Anyone who becomes as humble as this little child is the greatest in the Kingdom of Heaven" (Matthew 18:4, NLT). In Dallas Willard's book *The Divine Conspiracy* he writes, "Interestingly, 'growing up' is largely a matter of learning to hide our spirit behind our face, eyes, and language so that we can evade and manage others to achieve what we want and avoid what we fear. By contrast, the child's face is a constant epiphany because it doesn't yet know how to do this. It cannot manage its face. This is also true of adults in moments of great feeling—which is one reason why feeling is both greatly treasured and greatly feared."[3]

Just as children need fairy tales, we grown-ups need a story of truth to hang our hopes on. The gospel of Jesus Christ is the only true story genuine enough to interface with our honest doubts and fears, pervasive enough to respond to all the existential dilemmas of human adult life. That God would love sinners enough to send his Son to die for us, even in the midst of our sins, is a truth so profound, so far beyond our understanding, that at times, trying to believe it may have the feel of fantasy as we try to reconcile it with the circumstances of our lives. Yet it is the essence of absolute truth. Placing our faith in Jesus Christ throughout our everyday lives is not sweet-sounding make-believe or magical thinking. It's a truth-based, experiential, present-moment practice of intimacy with God that leads to the only solid foundation for the Christian's healthy self-esteem—God's unlimited, unqualified, undeserved love for human beings. Experiencing this kind of relationship is something we can *live* during these days of the Meantime even though we can't have the uninterrupted blissful union with God our hearts long for until we get to heaven.

Frederick Buechner said the gospel of Jesus Christ is "the fairy tale too good *not* to be true."[4] This is the discovery Valerie began to make as she experienced more moments in God's presence. She found that he was more interested in an honest relationship with her than whether she'd done everything right. Although Valerie would bear the natural consequences of her sins, as we all do, God's goodness was far bigger than her own badness; his forgiveness was far more pervasive than her promiscuity. His divine grace was extravagant enough not only to cover her most human weaknesses but to make something beautiful of them.

I once draped an elegant Battenburg lace cloth across a beat-up, distressed table and was surprised at how the contrast portrayed a faint reminder of the Incarnation. Suddenly the worn table—old, plain, fit for the junkyard—became unique, beautiful, more interesting for all its scars. God has always worked through the most unlikely people—the weak, needy, broken ones who know they can't clean up their own lives or make themselves look good.

Maybe you are like Valerie, who had always thought of herself as the black sheep of her family. Or perhaps you are more like me. I took the part of a "good girl" in my childhood years, trying hard to please Mother and Dad so they'd be proud of me, relishing the times I earned their approval. Unknowingly, I carried this mentality into my first marriage and then into my spiritual life. I began trying hard to serve God well enough to make him happy, to do enough, to learn enough, and to have faith strong enough that God would answer my prayers as I wanted him to and I would feel loved.

I began to study the Bible, go to church, and pray. My heart's deepest desire was to be a godly woman, wife, and mother to my two preschool-age sons. Confusion, disillusionment, and fear stacked up and culminated when my first husband left home and filed for divorce after I prayed fervently that God would keep our family intact. For a long while I denied my doubts, fears, and questions because they didn't align with my image of a strong, faithful Christian. I increased my efforts to be disciplined in prayer, study, and service, trying harder to fit the description of a successful woman of faith. Years later I discovered that I'd gone through lots of right spiritual motions and told myself that was what it meant to have faith, but somehow, in spite of all my good intentions, I'd missed God—his sovereignty, his love, and his presence in the ups and downs of real everyday life.

Strangely, Valerie and I came at God from different directions—she from the black-sheep stance and I from the "good girl" mentality—but we both ended up confused and discouraged. Each of us was in need of intimate life with the Lord, who wants only to be trusted and worshiped, not figured out with the human mind, like an Alfred Hitchcock mystery. We both needed to admit our idolatry and spiritual pride, to see that we were considering whatever was true of us (whether "good" or "bad") more profound than the infinite scope of God's character. Each of us had inner roadblocks to an intimate relationship with our divine Creator. As time went by, I found that this is a common problem among sincere Christian women, many of whom are deceptively trapped in forms of bondage that are hard to recognize because they look so right on the outside. But God looks on the inside, at our hearts' motivations, and we need to do that too.

Fairy Tale Faith is written to those who know they don't deserve to be loved by a holy God but who want to believe in the miracle that he does. Many women I talk with are finding that living a life of spiritual integrity and faith in God is simpler than they thought—simple, but not necessarily easy. Brennan Manning writes in *The Ragamuffin Gospel,* "We cannot will ourselves to accept grace."[5] Ultimately it is God's grace that empowers us with faith as we come into his presence. We seek him, he finds us. The amazing thing is that we really *are* ugly ducklings, the whole lot of us, and would always remain so except for one thing: For some reason we will never understand, God in his infinite mercy decided to love us here and now as his beautiful swans, and

> The amazing thing is that we really *are* ugly ducklings, the whole lot of us, and would always remain so except for one thing: For some reason we will never understand, God in his infinite mercy decided to love us here and now as his beautiful swans, and because he sees us that way, we are invited to *live* the invisible reality of who he says we are.

because he sees us that way, we are invited to *live* the invisible reality of who he says we are.

Fairy Tale Faith is an exploration of ways to live as a swan, experiencing present-moment intimacy with God and facing common obstacles that often block this intimacy. It addresses the deepest spiritual longing of a woman's heart—to know God through the experiences of today. Has it ever been hard for you to believe God delights in the pleasure of your company? Pastor and writer A. W. Tozer said, "God made us for Himself: that is the only explanation that satisfies the heart of a thinking man, whatever his wild reason may say."[6] Centuries before Tozer wrote those words, the Old Testament prophet Micah said much the same thing: "He has told you what he wants, and this is all it is: to be fair, just, merciful, and to walk humbly with your God" (Micah 6:8, TLB).

Not long ago I met a woman who had recently moved to Texas to make a fresh start in a new community. After silently suffering for years with serious marital problems, including infidelity, she and her husband felt painfully rejected when they shared their struggles with the people of their church. My new friend didn't know what to do. She had recently contacted an attorney about pursuing a divorce and had asked her friends at church to pray for her. "I felt as if I'd instantly turned into a leper," she said. "I don't know which was most painful—the condescending looks of disgust, the standoffish blank stares, or the callous sharing of much worse personal trials others had endured, ending with absolute guarantees that God would fix it all for us, just as he had for them."

My friend felt very alone. Nobody knew how to just listen and care before jumping in with unsolicited advice. The people she'd counted on to stand beside her through her trials now gossiped behind her back about her husband's unfaithfulness. "I even wondered briefly if all the stuff I'd believed about Christ's Spirit living in Christians had been a giant hoax. It was as if they couldn't handle it because we were struggling, even though we wanted to do the right thing."

After some time had passed, her husband requested a

transfer to Dallas. They joined a church community that welcomed them and loved and supported them through their crisis. A small group of friends listened compassionately and admitted that they had struggles too, though perhaps different ones, and provided sound biblical counsel and accountability. My friend and her husband vulnerably acknowledged their past sin, and in the atmosphere of love and acceptance, repentance followed. The couple began to heal in the company of accepting friends who knew that the admission of human weakness is what *qualifies* us for God's grace.

"So you found a kind of acceptance in the new church that your longtime friends didn't know anything about?" I asked.

"It's true that I found acceptance from them," she replied. "But that wasn't the main thing."

"What was the main thing?" I asked. Her remarkably simple response had taken me aback.

"They talk about the gospel as if it is something we need anew every day, and they live as if it is *true*," she said. This woman had found a group of people who were practicing their faith in such a way that they experienced the gracious presence of God one day at a time, not perfectly or because their faith was so strong, but vulnerably, because they knew their desperate need of God was what qualified them for his grace. As a result, they were somehow glimpsing the depth of Christ's love in a fresh way each day. And they were doing so gratefully because they knew it was something they did not deserve and could not earn. Because these people were learning deep spiritual truths for themselves, they wanted to share them with others who came into their midst.

Faith Is a Gift

• • •

IT IS BY THE HEART THAT GOD IS
PERCEIVED AND NOT BY REASON . . .
SO THAT IS WHAT FAITH IS: GOD
PERCEIVED BY THE HEART.

Oswald Chambers[7]

Without meaningful, soul-nurturing intimacy with God, we feel isolated and unlovable. Often someone, perhaps a mentor, spouse, or Christian friend, fleshes out some aspect of the character of God for us, enabling us to first experience acceptance and love from that person, as a stepping stone to our believing that Christ could delight in our company. As a therapist, one of my most sacred privileges is having the opportunity to affirm a woman's intrinsic value after hearing her tell of a dark experience in her life. *Am I okay? Will you reject me if I tell you how messed up I am?* she wonders as she tentatively exposes her humanness. When therapy works, it's largely because a counselor has responded to his or her client's need for emotional connection.

Dr. Larry Crabb wrote in his groundbreaking book *Connecting,* "People don't just have psychological disorders. They're suffering from soul disease."[8] He explains the vast difference between a prescription for a change of behavior and emotionally connecting in a meaningful way with others. It's like comparing problem-solving techniques to an intimate relationship. Finding solutions to problems may be helpful, but it doesn't address a person's need for real intimacy.

The same principle applies to a meaningful relationship with God. We all know that it's important that we learn Bible facts and principles of Christian living. But most of us are far less aware of our need to experience attunement with our heavenly Father—a sense of being wanted by him, accepted by him, welcomed into his presence, of his delighting in our company the way a new mother delights in cradling her infant child. If we don't think God likes us or if we think he's always mad at us, we don't have an understanding of the true character of God, and this will be an obstacle to closeness with him.

We can't create warm fuzzy feelings between God and ourselves, nor should we try. We can only present ourselves to him as seekers with open hearts and be willing to let go of the roadblocks to spiritual intimacy as God reveals them to us.

When Faith Seems like a Game

Sometimes the days that fall between our Once upon a Time and Happily Ever After can beat us up pretty badly and threaten to convince us that the gospel is just another of life's bad jokes. Jesus is one of the good guys, and he'll get us into heaven if we take him as our Savior, but in the Meantime, we're pretty much left to our own resources.

From the Italian film *Life Is Beautiful* we can learn some things about living a life of faith in God, especially when circumstances threaten to convince us we're foolish if we dare to believe the gospel really makes a difference in the present moment. Roberto Benigni plays the part of Guido, a young man who falls head over heels in love with a beautiful young woman named Dora. They first meet when Dora accidentally falls backward out of a hayloft into Guido's arms. "Buon giorno, Princessa!" he greets her. This nickname sticks with Dora for life—she is always to be his Princessa. Guido marries Dora, and they have a son, Joshua. After five years of fairy-tale life in Tuscany, something unexpected happens. Dora, Guido, and their small son are captured and taken to a concentration camp.

Guido intentionally pretends that it's a good place, turning a horrible reality into a simple game to build his son's hope and keep him safe. Guido tells young Joshua that the German officers are only "acting" mean when they shout angrily. He explains that he and Joshua are playing a game with a point system. Guido convinces Joshua to hide in the top bunk of the men's barracks all day while he is away doing hard labor. Each evening when Guido returns, he enthusiastically congratulates Joshua, announcing how many points the lad has earned toward the thousand points they need to win the game and receive the prize—a real army tank.

But one day Joshua hears the other children talking in the courtyard. "The boy said they will kill us and make buttons and soap out of us," he tells his father.

"Oh, no, Joshua," counters Guido. "He is only trying to throw you off track. You'll see."

"He says we get cooked in a furnace," Joshua persists.

"No. He's only trying to scare you, to make you give up, don't you see?" Guido convinces his son. Even though some people say Guido's explanation of "the game" is not true and that instead, Joshua and all the others will be killed, the little boy believes his father. Even on the days when the Germans frighten Joshua and some people say there is really no "game" at all, the young boy knows his father would not mislead him. Day after day Guido calms Joshua's fears and reassures him that everything will be okay, and the boy looks forward with anticipation to winning the prize at the end of the game.

Near the conclusion of the movie, the war is over, and the Germans evacuate the concentration camp, leaving few survivors. Little Joshua is hiding in a small cabinet, where his father left him with instructions to not come out until the game is over and all the people are gone. When all is quiet, Joshua opens the cabinet door, looks around tentatively, and steps out onto the ground. Just then a large army tank—a real one, with American soldiers—rounds the corner, just as Guido had promised. "It's true, it's true!" Joshua shouts, jumping up and down as he realizes full well that his father's words were true.

Although Guido sacrifices his own life in a final camp battle, Joshua and his mother survive. No doubt it took many years before Joshua could fully appreciate his father's contribution toward the happiest possible ending to their family story, especially during their days at the horrific concentration camp.

Do you long to live with Joshua's kind of faith—dependent on your Father's daily care and confident of his sacrificial love and his protection (even though it may not come in ways we would prefer)? Do you think God expects you to be strong and courageous without ever telling him when you're anxious or in need of his tender reassurance? Joshua believed what his father said because he knew his father's heart; he wasn't trying hard to believe in someone he didn't know intimately.

Like Guido, only far more tenderly and lovingly, God wants to reassure you that even when life deals you some bitter blows, his offer of intimate relationship is no trick. "Don't be afraid, for I am with you," he says in Isaiah 41:10 (NLT). "Everything will be okay, you'll see." Someday we will fully realize our "dream come true," the fulfillment of everything our Father has promised, just as young Joshua did. "It's true! It's true!" we'll rejoice, without any hint of insecurity, fear, or doubt.

On the complete fulfillment of our deepest desires, John Eldredge writes, "Have we really been poisoned by fairy tales? No, we've merely gotten the timing wrong."[9] We've not yet come to that Happily Ever After part of our Christian story, as we may have thought we would when we first met Christ as our Savior. That day is yet to come, when we finally meet Jesus face-to-face. In the Meantime we spend some of our days on the sunny hillsides and others in battles with Rodents Of Unusual Size. But when we face life's ups and downs in the company of Christ, we find that our very disappointments and broken dreams can lead us into deeper intimacy with him here and now.

Throughout our lives we encounter many perplexing dilemmas. Living in intimate communion with Jesus, whom we cannot see, *does* sometimes have the feel of a fairy tale. But the Prince of Peace is far too charming for a game of mere make-believe. The truths of the gospel are new each day, like morning mercies fairy-dusted across our lives, if only we have eyes to see. For those who know they need God and who seek him with their hearts, miracles await in the everyday moments of the Meantime.

• • •

ALTHOUGH THE WORLD IS FULL

OF SUFFERING, IT IS ALSO

FULL OF THE OVERCOMING OF IT.

Helen Keller[10]

RECOGNIZING THE TRUE
FACE OF THE KING

Understanding How You Relate to God

• • •

GOD FORMED US FOR HIS PLEASURE,

AND SO FORMED US THAT WE AS WELL AS

HE CAN IN DIVINE COMMUNION ENJOY THE

SWEET AND MYSTERIOUS MINGLING OF KINDRED

PERSONALITIES. HE MEANT US TO SEE HIM

AND LIVE WITH HIM AND DRAW OUR LIFE

FROM HIS SMILE.

A. W. Tozer[1]

One rainy evening two weeks before Christmas I stopped by the mall to pick up a couple of gifts. As I put up my umbrella and walked briskly to the nearest entrance, holiday colors danced in the puddles, reflecting the lights lining the storefront windows. Brushing past the crowds clustered around sale tables, I quickly cut a path to the mall area, where a long line of young children with their parents waited for their annual visit with Santa Claus. Casually scanning the young faces as I walked, I noted a variety of expressions: some wide-eyed with anticipation, others more reluctant. The child next in line was clinging to her mother's side, crying softly.

"No, Mama! I don't want to sit on his lap! I'm scared."

The young boy just behind her was a bit bolder. He walked up close to Santa, stared deeply into the jolly man's eyes, and pulled on his long white beard. "Cody!" shouted Mom. "Don't do that! That's Santa Claus, and you're supposed to tell him how good you've been all year so he'll bring you toys!"

Still standing by Santa's side, the boy grinned mischievously as he lifted Santa's beard to peer underneath.

"Cody, you'd better be nice!" Mom was now marching toward the child to rescue Santa as several parents began to chuckle, welcoming a moment of comic relief from holiday stress.

"But I want to see Santa's face!" the boy shouted in defense, now hoping to escape a public spanking. As the frustrated mom grabbed the boy and whisked him away, I doubted that this evening's experience would make it into their family album of memorable holiday moments.

Children are good at revealing the deep truths of human nature to grown-ups. The boy who wanted to see Santa's face bears a hint of similarity to the Greek Gentiles who approached Philip after Jesus' triumphal entry into Jerusalem for the Passover Feast. "Sir, we would like to see Jesus," they boldly announced (John 12:20). Crowds of people had gathered round, hoping to get a glimpse of Christ, and it is thought significant that the unlikely, unfavored ones—Greek Gentiles held a place of low status in their culture—were allowed to be present as Jesus foretold his coming death.[2] He didn't make a big deal of their presence, nor did he send them away, which highlights the universality of his sacrificial death on the cross: Jesus loved the people on earth—without exception—enough to die for them. Not only that, but each person could freely accept or reject a personal relationship with him.

Yet even though God loves us so lavishly, it can still be quite intimidating to approach him. Unaware, we may be like the little girl who was afraid to sit on Santa's lap: we're unsure what kind of image we'll find staring back at us when we look into his face. Is he an angry God, impossible to please, just waiting to scold us when we make our next mistake? Is he an absent God, not there for us when we really need him? Our concept of God can remain vague, like the faceless voice echoing from behind a blank screen in the Emerald City of Oz, after we've wearily stumbled down the Yellow Brick Road looking for him. Sometimes we unconsciously make up faces for God, forming images in our minds that match our own expectations and interpretations of him as we run them through the grid of our relationships and experiences in this fallen world. We don't always realize how we are fooled by the false faces we project onto our heavenly King. If we did, it wouldn't be the deceptive problem it is among so many of God's children.

Even though God loves us so lavishly, it can still be quite intimidating to approach him. Unaware, we may be like the little girl who was afraid to sit on Santa's lap: we're unsure what kind of image we'll find staring back at us when we look into his face.

One early spring day I was summoned by the Holy Spirit, unaware that I was about to confront my shockingly warped view of the character of God. Although I didn't know it, over the years, I'd mixed and matched my perception of God's nature with the behavior and faces of important people and authority figures in my life. If they were pleased with me, God must be happy too. If my prayers were being answered the way I'd asked, it must be a "God thing," and I was blessed. If they weren't, I must not have prayed enough, or prayed wrongly, or not been good enough, and God was mad at me. Determining whether he loved me or not on any particular day was about as precarious as picking petals from a daisy: he loves me; he loves me not. He loves me; he loves me not.

My husband, Frank, and I had spent a lot of spare time during our first years of marriage remodeling the country cottage we'd finally moved into just after my youngest son left home to enroll in a university. I felt my soul slipping into a Snow White death sleep as I searched for meaning beyond active mothering, work I could whistle a tune to, and a circle of Christian friends to get to know. My emotional coping skills dwarfed in comparison with the adjustments I saw looming before me.

We'd left the church we belonged to for more than ten years, a beloved pastor, and many friends, switching to a small congregation in a town nearer our home in the country. But before long we felt our spirits sagging under the oppressive overtones of the sermons, which emphasized God's wrath as a means of whipping us into holiness. From where we sat, it looked as if the pastor had fallen for legalism's mirage that we could go back to having things like they were before the Fall if only we wouldn't bite into that beautiful poisoned apple. Was this the picture of God I'd seen in the Scriptures? I wondered. Was God like this pastor, full of knowledge of the letter of the law but lacking in compassion as he looked down at us from a pulpit on high? As a natural-born rule keeper who knew she didn't always keep them perfectly, it had always been difficult for me to embrace the loving, merciful side of God, even though my former teachers and pastors had clearly presented God's grace and compassion.

Frank and I met with the pastor of the small church in hopes of establishing congenial grounds for our departing. To our dismay, we were given a sound scolding instead. Many of the people in the congregation became angry when we told them we were looking for a different place to worship. Some said God would punish us for leaving. As we limped away feeling isolated and condemned, I closed my Bible and placed it facedown on the bedside table, where it was to remain for several months.

Frank and I snuck into the back pew of a church once in a while and sat, looking on in a daze, listening to the singing, and then left, wondering where we fit in the body of Christ. Sometimes we gathered with our Christian friends at IHOP, where we listened to each other's stories, pooled our spiritual questions, reminded each other that we'd all seen better days with God and that heaven would be different.

Discouraged and confused during this "faith crisis," I sought counsel from Linda, a wise and deeply spiritual woman. She helped me inject some biblical truth into my thought patterns and align the negative self-judgments I'd reinforced following criticisms from the church members. But it didn't do much to heal the dull ache buried deep within my chest. Even the joy, love, and security I'd found in my marriage to Frank wasn't the cure-all solution I'd hoped would break through my resistance to accepting Christ's love with open arms.

What Qualifies Us for God's Grace?

Linda had often led me through prayer at the end of our meetings. We would close our eyes and picture truths from Scripture in our minds as we prayed: "The Lord your God is with you, he is mighty to save. He will take great delight in you, he will quiet you with his love, he will rejoice over you with singing" (Zephaniah 3:17).

"Can you see his face?" Linda would ask.

"No," I'd reply.

"When you look into his face, how is he looking at you as he sings to you and rejoices over you?"

"I can't see him close-up. He's faraway and faceless, sitting on his throne, but as I come closer, he disappears." Another week I might say, "No, I still cannot see his face. I see him sitting on a white horse, in a shining hooded robe, but the face is just a blank spot."

"It's okay," Linda would reassure me. "In his time and in his way God will reveal to you the truth of his character. In the meantime, we will keep seeking him."

Yeah, right, I would whisper under my breath, mentally mocking Linda.

As I curled up in a rocking chair that spring day on my deck, I wrapped myself in an old afghan my mother had once crocheted. Following nature's lead of shedding winter's white coat when springtime warms the earth, I also was ready to throw off a coat—one of shame and guilt that had tucked itself around my heart and held it captive since early childhood.

I recalled the words of Dottie Connor Bingham, dean of women at Dallas Theological Seminary at that time, who sat with me countless times at Grandy's, where we met for coffee, gently explaining Scripture verses about God's grace with assurance that they applied to people like me. "Don't you see? Our weakness and imperfection actually qualify us for God's grace." I didn't see it. Somehow the knowledge in my head had never made the eighteen-inch journey down into the bottom of my heart.

As I sat on the deck thinking back over my life—of trying so hard to make people happy, of trying to please God, of feeling ashamed and guilty because I could never quite succeed—a smoldering volcano of buried anger finally welled up and erupted. If the legalistic pastor was right, if God's grace was not true for me personally, I was ready to face it and stop pretending.

"God, haven't you punished me enough?" I demanded. "You say you love me? I don't feel loved!" I shouted into the sky. "The truth is, my sins are more real to me than you are!"

I sighed listlessly and began rocking in my chair as a battle played out in my mind. The character of God was on trial, and the only witness present was that familiar heavy feeling in my chest. Leafing through the book I held in my lap, I stared blankly at the pages as if searching for evidence that I should be allowed a blessed life, while mental mug shots from the past argued to the contrary.

Images of people I'd disappointed throughout my life arose from the cellar of my mind as I descended the stairway of time: our recent experience with the legalistic pastor, who scolded us because we didn't see things his way. My first husband, walking out the door as our two sons reeled in shock at the word *divorce*. Further back, my high school days as a cheerleader and homecoming queen, a playground scene in third grade, and finally, as a vulnerable little child.

A familiar four-year-old pushes a step stool over to the sink to wash the dishes while Mommy naps on her day off from work. Then there is Mommy's furrowed brow, tightened jaw, and wide eyes as she looks down, scolding me because I washed the dishes with cold water. I had tried to do something nice, but I hadn't done it quite right. Another memory floated into my mind, one of a "jewelry box" I'd created for my mother by smearing glue on the lid of a department store shirt box, sprinkling it with glitter, and topping it with the new birthstone ring I'd received for Christmas. I felt the familiar heavy feeling as I recalled finding the box in the trash the next evening after Mother had torn off the ring and crammed it back on my chubby finger.

"What's the matter with you? Don't you know that ring cost a lot of money?" Mother's words, coupled with her facial expressions, often sent me away to spend time alone in my bedroom wondering, *What's wrong with me?* Like all children, I didn't know how to discern that Mother was grouchy or working too hard or impatient. Instead, I internalized self-interpreted messages: *I messed up again. I'll never get it right.* Perhaps this was where those feelings of unhealthy guilt and shame had all begun. Maybe these were some of the memories I'd kept pushing below my consciousness because they clashed with scriptural truths I'd repeated over and over to myself and I felt guilty for doubting them. I was still trying to get something right.

As I sat rocking, a chilly breeze rippled across my arms, and I drew the afghan closer around my body. Just before the sun melted into the horizon like a giant golden ball, I began to sense God's presence. No audible voice spoke to me, and he didn't visibly appear. Yet I knew he was there. I felt a warmth unlike the rays of sunshine, more like a penetrating balm poured over my soul, massaging forgiveness directly into my heart. I began to feel comforted, blessed, as if someone were holding me close, "delighting in me, quieting me with his love."

In a moment of divine epiphany I would never again experience or ever be able to fully explain, the faces of the people I'd disappointed paraded through my mind in an instant. One by one, each was transcended by an image of Christ's radiant face. I closed my eyes, savoring the holy, penetrating gaze—strong, steady, compassionate. I wanted to hold that moment for keeps. I had never known such tenderness, and it was all such a surprise. Perhaps I'd expected God to answer my angry outcry with a scolding for not doing everything right or a "What's wrong with you?" But the warmth of his holy presence hovered around me in stark contrast to the negative messages I'd unconsciously repeated to myself over the years.

Suddenly I saw that the angry face of legalism projected by the overly strict pastor and some of the other authority figures in my life was *not* the face of God. This was not God's character. I had been trying hard to keep all the rules in an attempt to satisfy a demanding, punitive, critical God of my imagination. Until now I had had little true awareness of the heart of my heavenly Father. Now, instantly the distortion corrected, and I *knew* the truth of the words *Jesus loves me.* This wasn't a greater intellectual understanding of God's love in which I was taking what I already knew in my head to another level. This was the kind of knowing the psalmist talks about in Psalm 46:10 when he says, "Be silent, and *know* that I am God!" (NLT, italics added). The word translated "know" in this verse comes from the root word *yada,* which reflects a deep knowing that includes not just our minds but our senses as well. In these moments, I knew—deep in my soul—that Jesus loved me.

Before any people tried to love me, *he* had loved me first. I realized I'd *always* been blessed. Being blessed was being *his*—and everything that meant—or it was nothing at all. *Life itself* and his presence with me in it—this was the "God thing"—all of it. Nothing was beyond Christ's redemptive purposes and love.

God had lifted the glass lid of legalism and pride encasing my spirit for almost twenty years, since the time I'd first met Christ as Savior. I had been blinded to spiritual truth—had it all backwards. I'd always thought God's favor was about *my* faithfulness to him, that when I was faithful, I would know his favor. The "good girl" persona had won me some accolades in my family, at school, even at church, but it was never going to impress God. Something inside me shifted to rest on bedrock as I realized everything had always depended on *him—his* faithfulness, *his* righteousness, *his* justice, *his* love—not mine. Completely unaware, I had depended on my own abilities for obedience and faithfulness, which never quite measured up. Though I had called it trust, I was subtly deceived. Like the Pharisees who clung to the law when they had Christ right before their eyes, I had chased legalism's mirage across a desert of heartaches while an oasis of holy stillness and rest awaited in my own backyard.

It was my own distortion of the character of God that had condemned me to years of unhealthy shame and guilt. The convoluted deception had hidden in darkness until it was finally pushed too far, into the light of God's truth. The small-town pastor had finally made legalism's harm strikingly clear to me and exposed its contrast with the heart of God. At last the differences were irreconcilable. The pity of it all was that as time passed, I realized that the whip-cracking distortion the pastor related to—poor man—was the same one that had ruled me. What a lot I had expected of him and others whose approval I'd sought relentlessly over the years: a former employer, my first husband, my mother, and more. How I hoped each of them would see, as I did, the compassion with which the holy, radiant face of Jesus also shone on them.

With the help of mentors I settled into a more relaxed and joyful way of living my imperfect Christian life. I dusted off my Bible and returned to the spiritual disciplines I'd briefly abandoned, but now I approached them with eagerness and anticipation. A counseling supervisor helped restore my hope for an abundant life and encouraged me to enter graduate school, which I did, and later I became a therapist to other women and families. A kindly pastor offered an invitation to attend his church: "Just come and be yourself." With those words and the reinforcing acceptance we found in God's people, Frank and I were able to enter into church life more wholeheartedly. Healing would take time, and I would have to sort through my confusion about the character of God. But eventually I would see that *all* things worked together for good. Now that I knew that I was a loved woman, my heart was free to love others, to forgive them and bless them as I had been blessed.

God is faithful, and he uses even our painful experiences, rejections, and failures to draw us close to his heart; nothing is wasted or beyond his redemptive purposes. Our part is to keep seeking him. We're subtly off track if we think our messes and mistakes can shake God's steadfast goodness.

G. K. Chesterton said, "There is a great lesson in 'Beauty and the Beast' that a thing must be loved before it is lovable."[3] For the unlovable who are still hoping to be miraculously turned into those who are lovable, the gospel holds good news: it has already happened! If you can believe that, then you can experience the reality of the truths of God's character in your heart. God is faithful, and he uses even our painful experiences, rejections, and failures to draw us close to his heart; nothing is wasted or beyond his redemptive purposes. Our part is to keep seeking him. We're subtly off track if we think our messes and mistakes can shake God's steadfast goodness. The same is true if we seek an ecstatic spiritual experience, our own healing, our own faithfulness, or the answers we think God should give to our prayers.

Why had God finally broken through my emotional blockades and revealed his true character to me that day through a mental image of truth? Was it because I'd finally prayed sincerely enough or pursued him long enough? I can't know that. I don't understand how prayer works—I know only that it is good to pray. Was it because I'd found the Bible verse that would unlock my spirit at last? I don't know—I know only that it's good to know God's Word and that a slower, deeper drink of the Scriptures gradually heals wounded souls.

I can't order up spiritual epiphany any more than you can, and I don't understand why some people encounter such a moment while others plod along steadily without becoming discouraged. I know only that God is faithful to give each of us what we need. Most of all, I don't know why a holy God would call me his Beauty when I know I'm a Beast inside. But since he does, and I recognize the miracle, something in my heart has changed forever.

• • •

IN GROWING UP WE HAD NO EXPERIENCE
OF THE DIVINE PRESENCE WITHIN. . . . SINCE
WE DID NOT EVEN KNOW THAT GOD WAS
ACTUALLY PRESENT WITHIN US, WE HAD
TO LOOK ELSEWHERE FOR THE SECURITY,
AFFIRMATION, AND FREEDOM THAT ONLY
THE DIVINE PRESENCE CAN PROVIDE.

Thomas Keating[4]

ERASING YOUR DISTORTED IMAGE OF GOD

Many women I know *say* they believe Christ's nature is good and loving. They repeat the words of Scripture over and over to themselves but remain defeated and passionless because, as was true of me, the wounds to their souls have had an impact on their entire being, not just on their minds. The truth of the words must somehow come off the paper and be experienced, known in the biblical sense, as Christ ministers his presence to their receptive being—mind, body, and soul. In seeking God, we need to do more than read information about him and pray prayers to him, we need to experience his presence. In God's presence we are gradually healed from life's wounds, soothed and sustained, comforted and strengthened.

All of us are afflicted with tainted images of the face of Christ. It's just part of the contamination of human nature. But if our heads are full of misconceptions about the *character* of God, mixed up with memories and dim images of people and experiences in our lives, our efforts to become "transformed by the renewing of [our minds]" (Romans 12:2) can result in just more unhealthy guilt and shame because we're still not getting it right. As distortions persist, our interpretations of Scripture also become skewed to fit our perception of God.

Our rational stance is sometimes in disagreement with our true spiritual condition. We know that we *ought* to believe, think, do, or feel a certain way. We may even convince ourselves that we do. But it's so easy to rationalize and justify. On the other hand, if we try to face up to the fact that we truly aren't able to see God as a good king, that we have been wounded by life and now have a marred image of him, we may feel ashamed or condemned. Renewing ourselves in a relationship with God through his Word, his people, his presence—this is the task of the Meantime as we move from a fear-based relationship into a love-based relationship with him.

In a collection of devotional readings from the works of Augustine, David Hazard comments on the difference between the instant experience of salvation of the soul and the inner healing from the wounds inflicted by this life, including the warped ideas we pick up about God's nature. "Removing the cause [of the wounds] is only the first step in the cure. There is, in addition, the need to heal the spiritual illness itself. This is accomplished gradually, as you progressively erase the image of fallen man within and renew yourself in the image of God."[5]

Tara knew she *should* trust God, yet when she was honest, she had to admit she didn't. She'd tried positive thinking and choosing the "faith perspective," yet she found herself avoiding God and staying away from church, from Christian friends, and from personal prayer. Tara's marriage was in trouble. She was possessive and suspicious when her husband spent time away from her, repairing friends' computers and hanging out with guy friends. Both of them knew principles of good communication and conflict resolution, but as time passed, Tara and her husband had begun to feel like strangers.

As Tara and I discussed her current and past relationships, she discovered how her custodial grandmother's cruelty (physically forcing her to eat foods that gagged her, laughing at her when she hurt herself) had contributed to her avoidance of God. Tara would need to face the truth, express her feelings, and grieve the losses she had experienced before she could accept the reality that a holy, invisible God actually loved her, wanted her company, and was worthy of her trust, even though her grandmother hadn't been. Once Tara had confronted and untangled her distorted sense of God, she had a chance for a more abundant life as well as a healthier marriage. As she spent time being aware of God's presence, thinking of him as trustworthy, and intentionally opening her heart and soul to him as a loving God, her refreshed spirit breathed new life into the people close to her.

> Whatever is true of Christ surpasses whatever is true of our lives. It may be invisible truth, but it is ultimate, rock-solid reality.

New trials would come every day, as they do for all of us, but so would new mercies. She would experience fears, doubts, worries, and disappointments, but she would also experience God's comforting reassurance.

Brokenness and weakness mark our lives permanently, but strength beyond ourselves holds us together. This is how it is during the Meantime, because whatever is true of Christ surpasses whatever is true of our lives. It may be invisible truth, but it is ultimate, rock-solid reality.

Tearing Off the Masks

If your closest current relationships are painful and you don't understand why, it may be helpful to look at how you relate to God and people you love, today and in times past. As long as we have false faces fixed in our minds, our distorted expectations blind us to the real image of Jesus. Remember the little girl who didn't want to sit on Santa's lap? Who among us wants to crawl up into the arms of a God whom we expect to endlessly scold and shame us? Only when we find a way to pull down the masks and expose the impostors we call God can we see the true face of Christ revealed by the Holy Spirit and find freedom to relate to him as a loving God.

In Alexandre Dumas' classic novel *The Man in the Iron Mask,* the people of France learn a lesson about their expectations of kingly behavior as they mix and match the faces and character traits of a royal duo. King Louis XIV assumed the throne when his father died, but he was not a good king. He selfishly squandered money on extravagant pleasures while the people starved. Unknown to the public, Louis had an identical twin brother, Philippe, who had been exiled to avoid any possible feuding over the throne. Philippe's identity was kept secret even from himself, his face locked in an iron mask.

But Louis's selfishness went too far when he deceptively sent a young townsman to frontline battle and certain death so that he could steal his beautiful wife. This incident set off its own epic battle as the retired Musketeers reunited to rescue Philippe from his prison cell. Prisoner 64389000 was the only name Philippe had heard in years. The Musketeers gave him a crash course in the ways of royalty, teaching him to duplicate Louis' arrogant mannerisms, coaching him on hiding his own goodness in order to fool the public. France's only hope for a return to prosperity lay in replacing the cruel king with his good twin.

The secret switch takes place one night during a royal ball. Louis is defrocked and gagged, and Philippe is dressed in the royal garb and escorted back to the ballroom. As he approaches the throne, no one appears the wiser—until a dancing maiden falls and Philippe instinctively rises from his throne, rushes to her side, and stoops to help her up. *Are you okay?* his compassionate eyes ask.

A hush quickly falls over the ballroom, the orchestra stops playing, and the people stare at Philippe in utter shock. *This is not the behavior of our king! He would remain on his throne looking dignified!* Even the young maiden is aghast at Philippe's kind gesture, so unlike the character of Louis. Feigning his brother's arrogance, Philippe catches himself, rises, and waves his hand. "Continue," he commands. The music and dancing resume, but Philippe has failed at impersonating his brother. He is found out and thrown back into prison, but not for long. Philippe's compassionate response has awakened a near-dead longing in the French people's hearts for a good king. This time the Musketeers see to it that Louis has his turn in exile.

When the people in the story first saw the familiar face of their king and observed his atypical behavior, they didn't know how to respond. No doubt it all felt quite foreign, just as the idea of God's loving us may seem foreign if we've come to expect rejection, standards of perfection, and demands that we can never meet.

What kind of behavior do you expect from your King? If you find yourself avoiding God, fearing his punishment, approaching him only for directions, and unable to ask for what you need emotionally, is it possible that you are mixing and matching faces and character expectations with those of important people in your life, in either past or present relationships? Is your god the distant king who knows you only by a number? Does he walk about arrogantly spouting orders and expecting you to carry them out perfectly? Or is he the king who stoops to help you up when you fall, who can neither hide his goodness nor hold his heart back from loving you?

Jesus is the king who rejoices over you, quieting you with his love. He is the king whose kind face looks lovingly into your eyes every time you come to him, whether you perceive this to be true or not. He sees all the way to the bottom of your soul. He knows all of those sins for which you've begged forgiveness a thousand times and yet they remain ever before you. But to him they are forgotten, erased forever.

Sometimes we have to untangle the knots of confusion we may have tied together over the years, often beginning in childhood. We may say we believe that God is loving and good but our ways of relating to him reveal our hearts. As we grow more aware of God's grace through increasingly experiencing his loving presence and truth, our distortions of his character fade and we begin to see and trust his real character. When the marred images do reappear, we'll recognize them more quickly as frauds and return to the welcoming smile of our heavenly Father.

It is our imperfec-tions that quality us for God's grace.

Untangling our misconceptions about the character of God ultimately demonstrates that his strength surpasses our weakness (see 2 Corinthians 12:9) and that "God causes everything to work together for the good of those who love God and are called according to his purpose for them" (Romans 8:28, NLT). My friend Dottie was right; our imperfections *qualify* us for God's grace. When this truth finally penetrated my heart, I was able to give my mother the blessing I'd always been hoping for and waiting for her to give me. I now knew Jesus loved me, and not only that—he loved her, too! I was free to demonstrate compassion to her. There's more to this story, but I'll save it for a later chapter. For now I'll just say that in time, I began to realize that each disappointment and failure in my life became an opportunity to learn and grow.

As we are aware of the presence of God, we experience emotional healing. The Holy Spirit ministers to our feelings, transforming a child's (or a mother's) burdened heart into lightness and freedom. Plenty of trials will accompany us throughout the Meantime. Our hearts will still know an ache, but it will not be the emotional heaviness of unhealthy shame and guilt. Rather it will be a spiritual ache, a longing for Happily Ever After—that day when we will experience full intimacy and complete security in the embrace of our Lord.

Your experience in this life won't be the same as mine. It won't be the same as your friend's or even your siblings

raised by the same parents. We all have different temperaments, body chemistries, and levels of sensitivity, and all
of that is by God's design. But none of the details about
your history can make you unlovable when God has already
said he loves you. It's the invisible reality of the Incarnation—the miracle of Beauty and the Beast.

• • •

THE LORD JESUS HAS COME TO TAKE

FROM US EVERY YOKE OF BONDAGE AND

TO SET US FREE TO SERVE HIM IN THE FRESHNESS

AND SPONTANEITY OF THE SPIRIT, AND ALL THAT

BY THE SIMPLE SIGHT OF HIM WHICH THE

HOLY SPIRIT GIVES TO THE EYE OF FAITH.

Roy and Revel Hession[6]

DREAMING TRUTH
INSTEAD OF FANTASY

Learning to Stay Grounded in God

• • •

THEREFORE I ASK . . . THAT CHRIST MAY DWELL

IN YOUR HEARTS THROUGH FAITH; THAT YOU,

BEING ROOTED AND GROUNDED IN LOVE,

MAY BE ABLE TO COMPREHEND WITH ALL

THE SAINTS WHAT IS THE WIDTH AND

LENGTH AND DEPTH AND HEIGHT—TO KNOW

THE LOVE OF CHRIST WHICH PASSES KNOWLEDGE;

THAT YOU MAY BE FILLED WITH ALL

THE FULLNESS OF GOD.

Ephesians 3:13, 17-19, NKJV

I grew up in California, sinking my historical roots into the floor of the San Joaquin Valley in an agricultural community. The small town of Arvin, five miles from the setting of John Steinbeck's *Grapes of Wrath,* was nestled near the base of Bear Mountain, and in those days the air was clear. On a cold winter day I could see the purple folds flanking the slopes, and in springtime they turned green. Near Easter, poppies colored the foothills orange. We said the Pledge of Allegiance and sang "America the Beautiful" every morning at school.

Migrant workers came in the summertime to help harvest the grapes, and two of my uncles were packing-house foremen at Di Giorgio Farms. They brought us piles of Thompson Seedless grapes and wooden boxes of purple plums wrapped in crepe paper. My dad was a mechanic during his first years there; he and his best friend fixed cars for everyone in the town. Later he opened a radiator repair shop. The high school boys got summer jobs moving sprinkler lines to irrigate the fields of fruit and vegetables. The Mexican families grew Habanero peppers and ground corn from the fields to make tortillas. Every Christmas Eve my family ate homemade tamales for dinner, a traditional gift the women brought to my mother, who worked at the grocery store on Main Street.

One year we had an earthquake. Just before dawn my bed started shaking, and I thought it was my dad waking me up. But when I opened my eyes, he was not there. I walked into the kitchen, where all the canned food that belonged in the cabinets had been dumped out into the middle of the floor. My dad came to reassure me that everything was okay. We walked to the back door holding hands, and when he opened it, I saw wide cracks in the ground, telephone poles leaning sideways, and a brick building down the street toppled over like a house of blocks. The earthquake was bad enough to make the national news, and our relatives from Texas telephoned to check on us.

Behind our backyard stood an old oak tree, unmoved by the earthquake. Mature trees had weathered it well, and the tall palms lining old Highway 99 still stood. But most of the town would have to be rebuilt. I don't remember much about the reconstruction, only that everyone worked together. Arvin was a kind of embryonic community, nestled there in the fertile valley. I think we knew even then that an invisible God looked on as the majestic mountain stood in the background and the valley gave and took from us, steadied and shook us. In that community we learned many lessons about the basic needs of life: what it takes to stay grounded, the importance of roots, of giving and

receiving love, of working and playing together, and helping each other survive the tremors.

Although I watched people a lot from the outside as a
child and now I listen a lot to what's going on inside, it's still
these same basic elements that
help us stay grounded in God.

We need to be in communi-
ties that know and practice the
truth because we can't make it
on our own. Everybody needs to
share the fruits of their labors
and receive from the harvests of
others. We need to help and
pray for each other and trust
God together when the ground
shakes because he is the only
One who really knows what's
going on. God's love comes to
us through accepting friends,
shared prayers, his Word, and
his presence; these are all gifts he gives to us. How he
delights when we embrace his love with both hands, like a
wise mother delighting in watching her daughter open a
long-awaited gift.

> *For many Christians
> the most unbelievable
> part of the gospel
> story is that the most
> essential thing we can
> do in response to
> God's unconditional
> love is simply to
> accept it.*

For many Christians the most unbelievable part of the
gospel story is that the most essential thing we can do in
response to God's unconditional love is simply to *accept* it.
Accepting God's tender care is something we do continually, just as a plant absorbs nutrients from the rich soil surrounding it. It is not our acceptance of God's love that
makes it true; it was already true whether or not we believed
it or accepted it. Still, it is only as we take long drinks of his
life-giving love that we grow deep spiritual roots in him and
come into full bloom.

STAYING GROUNDED IN THE TRUTH

Oswald Chambers says that if we are to have "staying power
during the alarm moments of life," we have to be grounded
in God's basic truths.[1] We all know we should read the Bible

regularly. This is our root system. Some denominations award special pens to children for memorizing Scripture passages or have contests to encourage learning Bible facts. This is important because learning the stories in the Bible is like knowing your family history. The information provides the "mental furniture" on which we play out our life dramas and guides us in the ways of wisdom and spiritual prosperity. In our spiritual ancestors we can always find a character to relate to, whether we've behaved wisely or foolishly—it's all there in the family systems and personal profiles of the ancients, just as it is in our contemporary lives.

Many excellent studies are available. Gifted teachers have written guides for learning to accurately interpret God's Word and apply its truths to our lives. Insightful books about the power of prayer line bookshelves in many Christian homes and offer helpful models for including important elements of prayer and ways to practice them. We worship, study, pray, exchange ideas, and go to meetings in our church communities. Yet many sincere and disciplined Christian women still find themselves blocked from the kind of meaningful intimacy with Christ that others describe. Sometimes even when they're doing a lot of right things with the intention of serving God, their *focus* has veered off course, and they don't understand what has gone wrong.

Chesterton said, "The kingdom of God is most of all like a fairy tale. You are asked to do a small, insignificant thing and something magnificent and wonderful happens, not only to you but to the people you touch."[2] When we reach out and take the unconditional love of our Creator, something wonderful and transforming happens to us and to those around us. This is a simple act of trust, something small that we do, and insignificant in the sense that someone else has already done the hard part for us. Jesus has already loved us broken, messed-up sinners enough to die for us, and this is his continuous state of being—it never changes because he never changes. This truth applies not only for salvation of our souls. It is also the principle basis for ongoing intimacy between God and his children, once we have come into the Christian family.

The fantasy we're sometimes tempted to fall for is that *we* do the magnificent, wonderful part by being faithful and strong Christians and that's what makes the good life happen, when instead, God compassionately lets us be involved in a small way. Throughout the Scriptures we see that God graciously named men and women faithful, commended them as righteous. Read, for example, the list of heroes of the faith in Hebrews 11. Those people trusted God, and he made them faithful and righteous. The men and women in this "faith hall of fame"—Noah, Enoch, Rahab, and others— were called faithful and pleasing to God because they believed that "he rewards those who earnestly seek him" (v. 6). They lived in faith until they died, without ever receiving the things promised, only welcoming them from a distance. Their focus remained on God's faithfulness, not on their own. Those who get the emphasis backwards and hold to their righteousness and faithfulness as the central aim end up swelled with pride and legalism. Idolatry can sneak in the back door of our hearts and rearrange our affections, and in doing so, it can pull us off center from what should be the true focus of our seeking and rob us of gratitude to God for all he has done for us in bringing us into his family.

It helps to have practices in our personal spiritual lives that keep us grounded in the truth about whom we belong to and our connectedness to Christ throughout the day. Henri Nouwen suggests saying a simple, oft-repeated self-reminder: "I am a beloved child of God."[3] Brennan Manning tells of an elderly nun who had lived for years with painful wounds from childhood sexual abuse. As she repeated many times throughout the day, "Abba, I belong to you," she began to find healing and an assurance of God's love and acceptance.[4] It's sort of like saying the Pledge of Allegiance every morning. What we are doing is setting our loyalties straight for the day, reminding ourselves of the truth from moment to moment, and becoming attuned to God's presence as we know his welcoming embrace.

"Arrow prayers" keep us aware of God's presence with us as we go through our days. We can send them up while we're changing diapers, presenting a sales proposal, or anticipating a moment of great temptation. *Lord Jesus, I need your courage. I'm exhausted; please give me patience. Help me, Jesus. Hold me, Jesus. Thank you for the glorious sunset! I just can't seem to love this person; please love her through me.*

Our need for consistent prayer, grounding in the truth of God's Word, and reminders of who we are as God's children are some of the basics of getting into our hearts who we are and how much God delights in us, but we also need people with whom we can be real in an intimate setting. Do we really want to stand on shaky ground all alone or confine our celebration of living as children of God to solitary experiences? Solitude certainly has its place, as we will discuss in a later chapter, but women especially need to find Christian friends they can bare their hearts to without fear of judgment. Many people find this in small groups within churches. Some join support groups focused on specific issues where they can talk about their lives in an environment of trust and mutual respect.

THE FELLOWSHIP OF BROKENNESS

• • •

FATHER, I WANT TO KNOW THEE, BUT MY COWARD

HEART FEARS TO GIVE UP ITS TOYS. I CANNOT PART

WITH THEM WITHOUT INWARD BLEEDING,

AND I DO NOT TRY TO HIDE FROM THEE THE

TERROR OF THE PARTING. I COME

TREMBLING, BUT I DO COME.

A. W. Tozer[5]

Some time ago I found myself longing for a support group of accepting friends, a kind of AA chapter for Christians who are ready to acknowledge that we're all in recovery from the Fall and that we will be until Christ returns. I was looking for a group where a pastor's wife might share vul-

nerably about her husband's affair and find compassionate listeners instead of gasps, sermonettes, or formulas for
quick fixes. A nurse could ask for prayer support and/or
accountability if she'd gotten hooked on Valium. Our
hang-ups and those of people we love would take a backseat
to our mutual quest for hearts intimately connected to
Jesus.

"Just sit anywhere." Penny greeted me with a friendly
embrace when I arrived late at the first meeting. "We're
glad you're here." I'd decided to join a group of people
who gathered together one day a month to support and
pray for one another, share authentically, and explore and
practice spiritual disciplines.

At the front of the hall a cheery-faced woman stood
lecturing, writing on a flip chart as she went along. "Just as
we all have different personality types, we also approach
the spiritual life from different perspectives." Iris Pearce
was a woman I, along with many other friends, would grow
to love and learn from. "Now, I want you to write down
your fears, resentments, and hurts, making three columns
on the piece of paper in front of you," said Iris. "Then I
want you to share with the person on your left what you
have written down." *Just like that?* I silently questioned,
glancing anxiously at the person on my left as she looked
back at me through equally panic-stricken eyes. *Recognizing
my feelings is one thing, but telling a complete stranger about all my ugly
stuff before we even get to know each other?*

"I'm about ten minutes late, and I feel as if I'm walking
into the middle of a movie. What all have I missed?" I
asked the woman on my left.

"Not much," she said. "I think the leader just gets right
down to business."

"But first—" Iris interrupted our tense chatter—"first, I
want to show you my list." She quickly flipped to the next
page of the chart, revealing her list of fears, resentments,
and hurts. "As you can see, I have a lot of fears. I fear the
mission project will fail. I'm afraid of driving across town
in heavy traffic. I fear . . ." As Iris enumerated the items on
her fear list, I noted her apparent detachment from guilt

and self-consciousness, a hint that I might have found the group of people I was looking for. During the very first half hour of the meeting, Iris vulnerably, and with humor and wit, disclosed her fears, hurts, and resentments to us.

"When we have a lot of fears, we need God to give us faith," she said matter-of-factly. "When we are resentful, we need to admit it to God, and he will give us hope. We always need his love, but we especially need it when we suffer hurts, because his love heals." With the person on our left we spent the next hour sharing the condition of our souls as God had revealed it to us in that moment.

"Hi, I'm Cindy," whispered the woman beside me, forcing a smile. "I'm digging deep down, trying to be open like Iris is, but it's hard for me," she said.

"Oh, it is for me, too," I agreed, "especially when we don't even know each other." But once Cindy and I got going, it wasn't as hard as we'd anticipated to "spill our spiritual guts." Before the day was over, I learned that Cindy's son was involved in drugs and had cut off his relationship with her. He didn't answer her phone calls, and her letters to him came back marked "return to sender, address unknown." A couple of good friends had encouraged Cindy and her husband with stories of their loved one's drug problems and subsequent rehabilitations.

I would later learn how she had tried clasping her hands around the sure-sounding ring of others' success stories and then in prayer claiming certain recovery for her loved one too. But it hadn't worked. Months had passed, and nothing was changing. Cindy needed people to remind her that it was *God's* yoke that was easy—not hers; it was *God's* transformational process that could make things change, not hers. She needed rest for her weary soul.

Cindy and I openly shared our stories, disclosing our hurts and fears. Somehow, describing our dilemmas to each other clarified ways in which our hurt had grown into resentment and brought an awareness of our need for confession to the surface. Because of our mutual sharing, God looked a little bigger to both of us.

"Staying connected to God is what keeps me grounded,"
Iris said as she began our afternoon session. "Each morning
I turn over my heart, mind, and soul to God." This was Iris's
statement of surrender and her reminder that throughout
that day she belonged wholly to God. A clinical psychologist
by profession, Iris had started her group after learning that
practicing experiential intimacy with God through the use of
the Scriptures and classic works on meditation and prayer
greatly helped cancer patients cope with pain and hopeless-
ness. Her daughter's bout with bone cancer at a young age
had been the catalyst for learning, sharing, and developing a
ministry to cancer patients, which later grew to incude the
general public.

"First I pray as the psalmist did, 'Search me, O God,
and know my heart. Try me, and know my anxieties; and
see if there is any wicked way in me, and lead me in the way
everlasting.'[6] Then I sit still and just wait quietly." Iris
paused, as if to give us time to absorb what she was telling
us. "So far, there has never been a morning when I did not
have a list of anxieties. Some have grown into wicked
resentments; others have wounded me and become painful. This is what God is shining his searchlight on and what
I must tell him. I call this 'emptying the garbage.' "

Iris's openness revealed her trust in God, even for her
knowledge of what she needed to confess. She "emptied
the garbage" and opened herself up to the presence of
God, asking him for healing, picturing truths from the
psalms in her mind as she repeated the words. She also did
a lot of analytical study. But what she wanted to talk to people about was practicing a growing relationship with God,
being together as we came to meet him, and depending on
him to change us as we gathered around his feet like little
children. The validating experience of being seen, heard,
known, and accepted by other people encouraged us to
trust God together to do whatever fixing we needed. Just as
women often want their husbands to just listen to them,
not try to fix the problem, many Christians want to share
their struggles vulnerably and find listeners who will toler-
ate the uncomfortableness of their not having it all

together, offer compassion, and refrain from automatically offering unsolicited advice.

When we confine our relationship with God to only the accumulation of information about him, we may miss the experience of his presence or fail to realize that the *act* of adoring God is very different from merely *reading about* adoring him. If you sing it, you get closer to the real thing. We may say, "I confess my sins to you, Lord," but if we have no idea what specific sins we are entangled in, the same temptations may bite us from the backside day after day, year after year, and we'll never grow in the strength it takes to resist them. We all know that some temptations keep coming around anyway, so we need to be about growing in intimacy with God and experiencing the reality of his presence with us.

> When we confine our relationship with God to only the accumulation of information about him, we may miss the experience of his presence or fail to realize that the *act* of adoring God is very different from merely reading about adoring him.

This group of warm, accepting friends who wanted to experience the presence of God together helped us all hang on to the dream that even though *we* do not understand what God is up to in our lives or in those of people we love, *he* is worthy of our trust. Cindy wanted to trust God instead of clinging to the fantasy that she could control God's action in her son's life if she just prayed enough hours or fasted often enough or made sure she never missed her "quiet time." Our entire group prayed for Cindy's son over the next six months. We asked God to bring him home quickly and safely. We prayed for Cindy as she sought wisdom from God's Word, from mentors, and from people with a clear understanding of addictions.

But as Christmas came and went, Cindy's son's presents were left under the tree, then stacked away in the hall closet for a reunion she would keep hoping for. Cindy's prayers weren't answered in the way she wanted, at the time she wanted; in fact, Cindy was still waiting and praying at the time of this writing. But her hope has found a resting place beyond the desperation of human understanding— in God himself and in his truth, his presence, his comfort. Sometimes Cindy's emotions still come undone, like blackbirds flapping with no place to land, and she reshuffles through the circumstances or tries again to make contact with her loved one. *Isn't there anything I can do besides pray and wait?* she wonders.

When the ground shakes, we fall on our knees, where we fight bloody battles with the evils invading our lives and those of people we love. We hold hands with friends who are willing to hear our true stories, who will pray for us and with us. Sometimes it's our raw need of God that keeps us going.

• • •

HOPE IS HEARING THE MELODY OF THE FUTURE.

FAITH IS TO DANCE TO IT NOW.

Richard Alves[7]

THE GIFT OF UNEARNED ACCEPTANCE

• • •

THERE IS A REMNANT CHOSEN BY GRACE.

AND IF BY GRACE, THEN IT IS NO LONGER

BY WORKS; IF IT WERE, GRACE WOULD

NO LONGER BE GRACE.

Romans 11:5-6

As we look into the lives of spiritually grounded people, we see a few common threads woven into the fabric of their being. They are not impressive threads of perfectionism and achievement but worn strands of human pain and frailty. These are people who are able to see God's beauty beyond their own ugliness or beyond anything at all about themselves. They want most of all to live with integrity, yet they know they often fail. Surrounding themselves with sincere, authentic friends who take joy in their mutual imperfection, these folks pick each other up when they lose their footing and steady those around them until they're back on solid ground. When trials come, some even find ways to turn them into something good by sharing their struggles and offering their mistakes and failures for the benefit of others.

Henri Nouwen openly shared some of his deepest struggles in hopes of encouraging others, particularly in some of his later written works, *The Inner Voice of Love* and *The Return of the Prodigal Son*. He writes about groping in spiritual darkness when he felt completely disconnected from the heart of God and talks about a community of people who helped him rediscover the most basic truths and the joy of loving and being loved.

When prestigious positions at Notre Dame, Yale, and Harvard did not lead to the personal fulfillment he expected, Henri found himself consumed by a spirit of competition and an insatiable desire for status, which left him feeling quite alone and begging those around him for approval. Plagued with insecurity, he constantly questioned, *Do you like what I write? Do you like what I say? Do you think I'm okay?*

Henri finally turned to a community of mentally and physically handicapped people at L'Arche Daybreak, in Canada, who knew nothing about all the books he'd written or the important positions he'd held. They weren't overly impressed with him and instead wanted only to know, accept, and care for him. One night Henri missed supper because he had something else to do.

"Where were you?" his friend Adam asked the next morning. "You weren't at dinner, and we were expecting you!"

"Oh, I'm sorry," replied Henri, probably quite surprised and perhaps embarrassed.

"You didn't tell us you were not coming, so you should have been at dinner!" Adam persisted. What Henri's new community may have lacked in sophistication, competitive spirit, and stimulating intellectualization, they well made up for in transparency and authenticity. From his friends who had no need to either placate or manipulate Henri, he began to learn on a deeper level than he had ever known what it meant to be well cared for, not because he had done anything special but simply because he was a valuable member of the L'Arche community. The faces of handicapped people, full of welcoming affection and appreciation, finally led Henri Nouwen to a place where he could admit how empty his life had become and begin to embrace the unqualified, undeserved acceptance of God with open arms.

We won't find solid grounding in Christ when we base our sense of worth on whether or not we can impress others.

We won't find solid grounding in Christ when we base our sense of worth on whether or not we can impress others. Sometimes we find this out only when we are removed from an audience of people we can manipulate in some way. All of us will probably have moments when we feel God has abandoned us, even as Christ did when he cried out from the cross, "My God, my God, why have you forsaken me?" (Matthew 27:46). We can't deny the fallenness of this world or somehow fix things so that we always *feel* lovable in every moment. But we can practice the kind of faith that Paul Tillich described when he defined it as "the courage to accept acceptance."[8] Only when we can honestly admit our own ugliness to others and experience their acceptance can we know together how beautiful we all are to God and rejoice in his love, which makes it so.

• • •

THOSE WHO DON'T HAVE ANYTHING TO
PROVE OR PROTECT CAN BELIEVE THAT
THEY ARE LOVED AS THEY ARE. BUT WE WHO HAVE

SPENT OUR LIVES ASCENDING THE SPIRITUAL
LADDER OR SOME OTHER LADDER CAN'T HEAR
THE TRUTH. FOR THE TRUTH ISN'T UP AT THE TOP,
BUT DOWN AT THE BOTTOM. AND BY TRYING TO
CLIMB THE LADDER WE MISS CHRIST, WHO
COMES DOWN THROUGH THE INCARNATION.

Richard Rohr[9]

STAYING GROUNDED YIELDS REST

• • •

COME TO ME, ALL YOU WHO
ARE WEARY AND BURDENED,
AND I WILL GIVE YOU REST.

Matthew 11:28

Reading the Psalms and other favorite Scripture verses, spending time with our spiritual family, remembering where our loyalties lie, writing brief prayers or poems, listening to good music, and spending time in nature are things that help some women I know stay grounded in God.

A single mom I'll call Barbara lost her job just after finding out that her twelve-year-old daughter had leukemia. She needed not only employment but also answers about her daughter's future. Would her daughter even be alive a year from now? How would Barbara pay all the medical bills? Friends rallied around Barbara with support, but for her, an introverted lover of nature, it was time to retreat to the lake for spiritual refreshment, taking along a journal and her dog. Sliding her toes under the mud on the shore, watching sunlight shimmer on quiet waters, smelling the trees, and watching the birds pressed Barbara into her spiritual roots and gave her renewed hope, and she wrote these lines:

Sink me down, deep into the dirt,
Beyond my fears, beneath my hurt,
Sink me down, past what I can see,
Into the depths of holy mystery,
Sink me down, pull me to Thy roots,
Into Thy truth, to bear Thy fruits.

For right now, Barbara remembers she is not alone and stops shaking. Tomorrow will have its troubles, but in this moment, if she squints her eyes into narrow slits, the light rays bouncing off the lake look like fireworks against a midnight sky. Her dog is smiling and pulling at the hem of her walking shorts, inviting her on a chase, and as she runs, the smell of cedars near the shore drifts across her path and sticks in her memory for tomorrow's needed refreshment. And life does go on.

Sometimes we cannot even know whether or not life will go on, at least not in the way we've grown accustomed. The Texas branch of the Hamilton family (my dad's relatives who didn't move west) gathered together a year ago to pace the hallways at Baylor Hospital's intensive care unit. A tidal wave of grief was about to hit our shores.

As the elevator door opened and Frank and I stepped into the waiting room, we met a sea of familiar faces of Greenville townsfolk. Making our way through the crowded room, we exchanged hugs and tears with old friends and family, finally reaching out to embrace Nancy Kate, my cousin "Sonny's" wife.

"The doctors still aren't sure exactly what happened," Nancy Kate said. "His bypass surgery went just fine, but then this morning for some reason he just stopped breathing. They gave him a shock treatment and hooked him up to a ventilator. Since then, he hasn't regained consciousness. . . ." Choking back tears, she melted into Frank's arms, sobbing.

My mind traveled back three days earlier when Frank and I visited Sonny before his surgery: I recalled his warm smile as he sat on his hospital bed in burgundy satin pj's, his affectionate greeting—"Hello, Cuz"—that I'd grown to love. It was hard to believe that my closest extended-family relative, known as the "Candy Man" at church and "Ham" to everyone in the Greenville community, now lay unconscious and that everything about his future was uncertain.

"Hello, Frank. Hi, Brenda." Sonny's boyhood next-door neighbor, Glen, came to hug us, his eyes red and his gray face reflecting hollow shock. As I looked around the room, I heard Vicki, another lifelong friend, softly reading the Twenty-third Psalm as her husband, Larry, stared, trancelike. People were everywhere, slumped in the chairs lining the waiting room, sitting cross-legged on the floor, crowding into the room far past its posted capacity. Sonny's loving heart was deeply rooted into so many people in his church and in the small community, and everyone just wanted to be together.

Over the next few days, friends and family waited, hoped, prayed, read comforting passages from the Bible to one another, hugged, cried together, and told affectionate stories about Sonny. Occasionally we laughed. People left the hospital for a few hours of sleep and returned with doughnuts, lots of coffee, and foot-long sandwiches to share. Pastors from the town came and prayed over Sonny, asking God for healing.

Why had Sonny stopped breathing? Was there a complication because of his diabetes? No one knew for sure. There were tests and retests; then his liver-function level dropped. A brain scan showed minimal activity, and finally the doctor suggested that the family consider turning off the ventilator to see if Sonny had any life left in him. Nancy Kate, her three children and their spouses, Frank and I, and Aunt Joella, Sonny's eighty-seven-year-old mother, gathered around the hospital bed as friends clustered in the waiting room to pray. If Sonny's brain waves had ceased and he could not breathe on his own, we would have to accept the fact that he was no longer with us.

As we held hands and prayed, the breathing machine was turned off. Sonny's chest lay still and flat. Nancy Kate began to rub his arm; then she whispered coarsely, "Come on, Ham, breathe! You can do it!" She continued rubbing

Sonny's lifeless arm, then his chest, his face, as her whispers gave way to groanings, "Oh Ham, please, breathe!" But his body lay quiet, lifeless. We grabbed each other and held on tight, the way people do when they lose someone so dear. Deep heart-cries echoed off the walls of the small room as we all let go of what we could not keep. Together, we had to bear a great loss.

When the room grew quiet, Sonny's daughter, Cindy, looked at Frank. "Would you lead us in 'It Is Well'?" Frank wiped away his tears and cleared his throat, and we joined hands, hearts, and voices. The sea billows were rolling, and somehow in the midst of all this grief, the deepest loss most of these people had ever known, we needed to sing. We were anxious, heartbroken, heavy laden, and somehow we had to keep going. We had to remember that Sonny had gone on to heaven ahead of us; we had to tell our friends, plan a funeral, get some rest.

Perhaps it was in a time of anticipation of the next life that Augustine once wrote these words:

> Let us sing alleluia here on earth, while we still live in anxiety, so that we may sing it one day in heaven in full security. . . . We shall have no enemies in heaven, we shall never lose a friend. God's praises are sung both there and here, but here they are sung in anxiety, there in security; here they are sung by those destined to die, there by those destined to live forever; here they are sung in hope, there in hope's fulfillment; here, they are sung by wayfarers, there by those living in their own country. So then . . . let us sing now, not in order to enjoy a life of leisure, but in order to lighten our labors. You should sing as wayfarers do—sing, but continue your journey . . . sing then, but keep going.[10]

In the coming days we shuffled through old photographs and listened as Glen and Larry told fond stories of their boyhood adventures with Sonny. We all laughed and cried and ate together. We hugged and prayed and read the Bible to each other. Over a thousand people came to Sonny's funeral. Six pastors officiated, and Frank sang the solo version of "It Is Well with My Soul." With God's help, everyone kept going, and Christ's love filled us full of his goodness.

We all have to endure trials and losses; we lose our footing and need our friends' helping hands. Especially during the "alarm moments" we return to basic truths, remember our roots, and hold each other up. The illusion that we can control things through exercising our faith is most alluring when there's most at stake. I, for one, would prefer to enjoy crystal clarity about what God is doing in those alarm moments and receive God's blessing in terms I can understand, but those things are to come later. In the Meantime, an invisible, majestic God stands watch over us, coloring the landscapes of our lives in hues of his own choice. We pass through peaks and valleys, life steadies and shakes us, and God's unchanging love is ours for the giving and taking.

• • •

SPEAK TO ONE ANOTHER WITH PSALMS,
HYMNS AND SPIRITUAL SONGS. SING AND
MAKE MUSIC IN YOUR HEART TO THE LORD,
ALWAYS GIVING THANKS TO GOD THE
FATHER FOR EVERYTHING, IN THE NAME
OF OUR LORD JESUS CHRIST.

Ephesians 5:19-20

UNLOCKING THE DUNGEON OF SELF-HATRED

Trading Self-Image for God-Image

• • •

OUR OWN COMPOSITE EXISTENCE IS NOT
THE ANOMALY IT MIGHT SEEM TO BE,
BUT A FAINT IMAGE OF THE
DIVINE INCARNATION ITSELF.

C. S. Lewis[1]

As the golden sun rises in the red sky above the Pridelands, the animals take their places along the valley floor in preparation for the royal welcome of the newborn son of the Mufasa, the lion king. Rafiki, the tribal wise man, holds young Simba high overhead in ceremonial presentation as the animals bow low. It is a moment of great joy.

Simba grows to love and respect his father as he learns the ways of honor, prosperity, and safety. Long days find father and son frolicking across the plains as Mufasa teaches Simba life lessons. "You must never go there," commands Mufasa, directing his son's attention to a dark region of gray, dead-looking trees in the distance. At first Simba complies, but after a short while he grows curious, wanders into the forbidden territory, and soon finds himself surrounded by ravenous hyenas. His father rescues him, but later Mufasa is trampled to death when his power-hungry brother, Scar, secretly pushes him off a cliff and into the valley during a stampede. Scar now seizes the chance to connive his way to the throne by blaming his innocent nephew for the king's death.

As the weeping Simba crouches over his father's dead body, Scar hisses bitter accusations: "What have you done? It's your fault!" Although Simba tries to explain that the accident was not his fault, Scar doesn't let up. "Run away and never return!" he commands. Filled with shame, guilt, and self-blame and operating under the delusion that his mother, family, and friends will be better off without him, Simba flees to the problem-free land of Hakuna Matata (no worries). For many months he distracts himself from any thoughts of his painful past by enjoying a carefree life-style with his new fun-loving buddies. Then one night Rafiki pays Simba a visit. It had been so long since the young lion had seen the wise baboon that he did not remember him. "Who are you?" he asks.

"Who are *you?* That is the question," replies Rafiki, quickly adding, "I know who you are—you're Mufasa's boy!" Simba follows Rafiki to a special place where he is to encounter the living spirit of his father. The time has come for him to claim his rightful place as ruler of the Pridelands. As he looks down into a pool of clear water, he sees a reflection of himself staring back. But as he gazes deeper, the image of his face slowly transforms into Mufasa's. The once-so-familiar and deeply beloved voice of Simba's father echoes across the dark blue sky.

"Simba!"

"Father?" replies Simba tentatively.

"Simba! You have forgotten who you are and so forgotten me. Simba, you are more than what you have become."

"I'm not who I used to be," Simba protests.

"You are my son," the voice answers, undaunted.

"Remember who you are. Remember. Remember. Remember."

There's a thick slice of reality in *The Lion King* if we care to gaze deeply into the meaning of knowing and remembering who we are. Have you ever been through at least one identity crisis? Have you listened to the voices of the Uncle Scars in your life when they blamed their darkness on you? Or worst of all, have you blamed yourself and taken on unhealthy shame you were not built to handle as you believed lies rattling around inside your head?

The attributes of the true self don't have their basis in what others think of us or even in who we think we are but rather in the person God knows we are.[2] Just as Simba lost track of the purpose of his life after his father was killed, we may lose our way on the path God has prepared for us. Sometimes when others accuse us, we need to learn to stand strong against unjust criticism. But far more subtle and deceptive than others' negative (and sadly, quite common) evaluations of us are the distracting, dark inner voices reflecting a battle between our true self and a condemning internal critic. *What have you done? It's your fault!* the critic accuses, shackling its victim and leading her down a dark hallway to the dungeon of self-hatred.

The attributes of the true self don't have their basis in what others think of us or even in who we think we are but rather in the person God knows we are.

—Iris Pearce

The debate over the role of self-image is as common among Christian counselors as it is among humanistic self-help and self-esteem experts. Dr. Archibald Hart, president of the American Association of Christian Counselors (AACC), acknowledges the complexity of the issue and describes this internal measuring of one's personal esteem this way: "Humans have the capacity for *self-awareness,* and out of this awareness of the self, there is a tendency to be *evaluative.* We pass judgment on what we see in ourselves and thus develop what can best be described as *an attitude of the self toward itself.*"[3] At its worst this "attitude of the self toward itself" can be loaded down with unhealthy self-condemnation that is often tricky to identify because it's easy to mistake it for the biblical ideal of "dying to self."

A Portrait of Self-hatred

• • •

OUR IDOLS BECOME THE MEANS BY WHICH

WE FORGET WHO WE TRULY ARE AND

WHERE WE TRULY COME FROM.

John Eldredge[4]

Paula and her husband had just returned from a retreat for missionary couples. The retreat coordinators had recommended that Paula seek professional counseling to address her negative self-image. "I don't know what's wrong with me," Paula told me. "I was once so excited about the ministry. I couldn't wait to get to Africa and tell people about Christ. I've tried so hard to be a good servant for God. But to tell you the truth, I've lost my enthusiasm to the point I'm not so sure I know anything at all about him myself!"

Over the next weeks Paula described ways in which she had tried to always put others' needs ahead of her own, serving in whatever way she was asked in an effort to do as Jesus said in Matthew 16:24: "If anyone would come after me, he must deny himself and take up his cross and follow me." But somewhere along the way she had lost track of what she once believed was her life purpose. She had lost the closeness she had once experienced with God and was now often haunted by suicidal thoughts. As Simba did, she took false accusations to heart and thought maybe her family would be better off without her.

"Paula, what are some of the internal statements you are saying to yourself, perhaps judgments or evaluative statements, as you go about the business of meeting others' needs?" I asked one day. Paula couldn't respond. She was not aware of her inner dialogue. So I asked her to try to discover her self-talk, trusting God to expose some of the facets of her inner critic. (You may attribute these negative inner messages to the voice of Satan, and that is certainly where the lie is coming from. Whether you call it negative self-talk or the voice of Satan, you need to recognize that you're being deceived and stop listening to that inner negative criticism. Those who struggle chronically with this problem may find that the term *self-talk* helps them to accept responsibility for *believing* lies, admit that they can't stop believing them by themselves, and trust Christ with their burden instead of inflicting further shame on themselves.)

Several weeks passed. Then one day Paula brought a list of statements she had discovered as she scanned her heart for stacked-up shame. Her list looked something like this: *You stupid woman! What ever made you think you had what it takes to succeed at being a missionary? Look at you! You're an insecure, fearful woman—what do you know about life in Christ anyway? When was the last time you really helped anyone? Who are you kidding!* As Paula read her list, her sad eyes reflected her own wounded spirit within.

"I know this is just the voice of Satan and I shouldn't listen to him. But I can't seem to stop, so then I'm guilty of yet another sin!" she said.

Ultimately Paula, as well as many others who become victims of their own self-hatred, had to face the same question Jesus once addressed to a lame man: "Do you want to get well?" (John 5:6).

If this question seems a nonissue to you or if overcoming negative thoughts with a positive outlook comes easy for you, perhaps you've never known the comfortable benefits of the dungeon of self-hatred. Imprisonment does offer some advantages. If you cling to your pallet in your cell, making idols of your accomplishments, your attempts at people pleasing and perfection, you'll never have to take on the task of becoming the person God has truly sent you here to be. You won't have to learn to develop respect for yourself as one of God's children sent to earth for a purpose. Nor will you have to learn new skills such as speaking the truth in love, stating your own needs and limits so that you can truly live for him. The gruel of self-hatred, though lacking in flavor, can become so familiar that it's more appetizing than the idea of feasting on a hearty mix of accountability and spiritual wellness.

After listening to Paula enumerate about a page and a half of statements from her inner critic, I finally leaned forward to make eye contact with her. "If a good friend of yours had just made some big mistake and you knew about it, would you scold her the way you do yourself?" I asked.

"No," Paula said without hesitation.

"Not even if it was the sin you consider most insidious of all sins?" I persisted.

Her eyes brightened. "No, I wouldn't."

"What do you think you might say to your friend?"

"I'd probably reassure her of God's forgiveness of confessed sins. I'd say, 'You'll do better next time,' or something like that."

"Oh. That sounds a bit like Jesus' telling the woman caught in adultery that he did not condemn her and she should be on her way, moving toward doing better next time."

"Yes, I suppose so," Paula agreed.

"What right do you have to judge a child of God more harshly than Jesus does?" I asked.

Paula was taken aback. "What right do I have?" She repeated my question with a puzzled look. "Well, I don't know." For an instant Paula appeared to catch a glimpse of the twinkling lights of Wonderland as she took a peek through the keyhole to spiritual liberty. Then her smile faded, and she lowered her gaze, "But I'm *not* the woman Jesus forgave. I'm not even sure I'm forgivable." There would be no tea party for Paula. At least not today.

Over the years Paula had been lured far from home on her Father's pridelands and had become far less than what he had imagined when he created her. She had listened to the deceptive voice for so long that she likely couldn't picture what her life would be like without its nagging accusations.

Only when the deep ruts of self-rejection are exposed for what they are do we even have the option of repentance. Henri Nouwen says, "The worst of all sins is the sin of self-rejection."[5] It is the disguised enemy many Christians remain fiercely committed to and so block their healing from deep life wounds from the past. I hoped Paula would allow Christ to break through her obsession with her own unworthiness and began to pray that she would *want to* get well.

SEEING THROUGH GOD'S LOOKING GLASS

• • •

IN THE EYES OF THE MASTER WE HAVE

FAILED, WE DETECT THE INFINITE COMPASSION

OF THE FATHER AND SEE REVEALED

THE HUMAN FACE OF GOD.

Brennan Manning[6]

We may not readily recognize self-rejection as sin, but it is, because we are God's children. At the core of faith is our need to look past ourselves, our problems, and the image we may have created of ourselves to the image God has of us. As we peer into God's looking glass, we see beyond the mere reflection of ourselves to the self he knows we are—"a faint image of the Divine Incarnation itself" as C. S. Lewis said. Only then can we let go of the critical view that may be deeply ingrained in us, perhaps even as a result of former significant relationships, and gradually trade in our self-image for a unique image of God living inside us as we dwell in his presence.

At the end of the seventh chapter of Romans, Paul has gone to great lengths to describe his internal battle with sin: "Oh, what a miserable person I am! Who will free me from this life that is dominated by sin?" (v. 24, NLT). Then, instead of getting stuck in self-condemnation, he acknowledges the reality of the battle and his wretchedness and then looks beyond himself, beyond reason, beyond laws and his best—though unsuccessful—efforts to keep them, to see the solution. "Thank God! The answer is in Jesus Christ our Lord"(v. 25, NLT).

G. K. Chesterton describes a similar way of looking

beyond himself, beyond facts and reason, to find paradoxical solutions to everyday problems: "I am not concerned with any of the separate statutes of elfland, but with the whole spirit of its laws, which I learnt before I could speak, and shall retain when I cannot write. I am concerned with a certain way of looking at life, which was created in me by fairy tales."[7]

This spirit of the laws of fairy tales that Chesterton writes about is something beyond reason and remarkably akin to the truth that Jesus Christ loved sinners enough to die for us. In fairy tales, story after story illustrates this principle: it takes a kiss to turn a frog into a prince. Someone must *see* a beast as beautiful before it turns into a beauty. In the same way, men and women must know their need for grace before they experience the depth of God's love. Just as the apostle Paul could not find it in himself to keep the law no matter how hard he tried, we will never be able to handle our own guilt no matter how much we punish ourselves; it's just not one of our options. And if we hang on to our shame and guilt, they become toxic. As one of my wise eight-year-old friends said, "Guilt is like brussel sprouts. It makes you want to throw up, and you feel much better once it gets outside you."

If we hang on to our shame and guilt, they become toxic. As one of my wise eight-year-old friends said, "Guilt is like brussel sprouts. It makes you want to throw up, and you feel much better once it gets outside you."

Paula was now facing the challenging choice of whether she would cling to the security of her cell pallet or arise and begin a healing ascent from the pit of despair. Did she want to get well? If so, she must take responsibility for her fierce commitment to the sin of self-hatred and trust that Christ did indeed dwell inside her as a faint image of the divine, just waiting to be revealed. She wrote:

You looked at me
Through the mirror today,
I saw you—you saw me.
Your accusing eyes
Brought to mind
So many memories
from the past.
Please, can't we just be friends?

When I'm hurt, you tell me to
"shut up and take an aspirin."
When I'm trying hard,
You say, "You're still not perfect."
And when others reject me,
You get out your whip,
And hiss at me,
"What did you expect?"

Cruelty is no cure for self-hatred.
It only unleashes
an attack of anger on me,
And stockpiles an arsenal
Of resentment toward others.
Aren't you ready to give up this feud?
I'm tired. Weary. Heavy-laden.

Then comes Jesus
To join our hands together,
Disarmed, we are silenced.
We see each other
Through a new looking glass.
The wicked witch in me
Is quieted at last
By his gentle snow white love.

As time passed, Paula decided she had been emotionally crippled long enough. She wanted to get well, to trade in her poor self-image and become the person God knew she was. She began by claiming her birthright anew each morning, replacing the cruel inner scoldings that had riveted her emotions for so many years with a fresh reminder of the truth of her identity: "I am a beloved child of God." No matter what happened through the day, that truth would not change. Now Paula was discovering the *true* meaning of "deny yourself" (give up your idolatrous magnification of your faults, turn over your self-indulgent, self-pitying, people-pleasing, shame-imprisoned self), "pick up your cross and follow him" (look at Jesus and he will reflect to you your true self in each moment).

As Paula began to see herself as one of God's children, no more and no less important than all the others, she gained perspective. She practiced turning her guilt over to God instead of clinging to self-pity or trying to shame it out of herself as she had done for so long. The grudge she stubbornly held against herself unaware had blocked her from meaningful connection to God. Until she discovered this, she was completely out of touch with her true self—the person God knew she was.

Paula confided in her husband that even though she wanted to return to the mission field, she would need some periods of privacy. She had also realized that the style of ministry she had felt compelled to practice in the past—passing out food in the cafeteria line and teaching children's classes—did not match her spiritual gifts. She was much more suited to visiting the sick and empathizing with the hurting, and when she did these things, she "felt God's pleasure" the way Olympic runner Eric Liddell did when he ran, in the film *Chariots of Fire*.

Paula's husband eagerly agreed to the changes, having sensed the new freedom in his wife's spirit. Even though some of the people who had greatly admired Paula's tireless practical service at the mission appeared to be disappointed because her "new self" didn't fit their description of missionary life, it did fit God's design for her. As my exposure to Paula and her inner battles with self-condemnation came to a close, I knew she would influence others who would catch the excitement of walking in freedom, accepting themselves, by God's design, as the uniquely imperfect beings we all are.

• • •

LET'S JUST GO AHEAD AND BE WHAT
WE WERE MADE TO BE, WITHOUT ENVIOUSLY
OR PRIDEFULLY COMPARING OURSELVES
WITH EACH OTHER, OR TRYING TO BE
SOMETHING WE AREN'T.

Romans 12:6, *THE MESSAGE*

OUT OF THE DARKNESS, INTO THE LIGHT

• • •

YOU'RE HERE TO BE LIGHT, BRINGING
OUT THE GOD-COLORS IN THE WORLD.
GOD IS NOT A SECRET TO BE KEPT. . . . NOW
THAT I'VE PUT YOU THERE ON A HILLTOP,
ON A LIGHT STAND — SHINE!

Matthew 5:14-15, *THE MESSAGE*

When I read Brennan Manning's book *Stranger to Self-Hatred*, I knew that Brennan, like G. K. Chesterton, knew something of that "way of looking at life created [in one's heart] by fairy tales." Brennan vulnerably writes about his own formerly recurring battle with self-hatred and how he was set free, in the following paraphrased summary from his book:

> The subtle dominion of self-hatred had returned and I was back on the roller coaster ride of perfectionist depression, neurotic guilt, and emotional instability. The despotic power of my idealized self and the nagging litany of "I should have, I could have, I ought to have, why didn't I, why did I" persuaded me that my life and ministry were vitiated by vanity, insensitivity, and self-centeredness. Jesus set me free. I was reading the

[daily lesson] of the washing of the feet in John 13. Suddenly I was transported in faith into the upper room and took Judas's place among the Twelve. The Servant had poured water from a pitcher and reached out to wash my feet. Involuntarily I pulled my foot back. I could not look at him. I had betrayed the vision, been unfaithful to my dream, and thus unfaithful to his plan. He placed his hand on my knee and said, "Brennan, what these years together have meant to me. You were being held even when you didn't believe. I was holding you. I love you, my friend." Tears rolled down my cheeks. "But Lord, my sins, my repeated failures, my weaknesses . . ." "Brennan, I expected more failure from you than you expected from yourself. Nothing pleases me so much as when you trust me, when you allow that my compassion is bigger than your sinfulness."[8]

Do you know this Jesus that Brennan speaks of, who expects more failure from you than you expect from yourself? Only Christians, in the strength of Christ and not ourselves, have the ability to look at sin that resides within and not only survive but actually prosper and grow because of bold honesty. The irony is, when we are most aware of our own ugliness, we are free to discover and appreciate the beauty God has created inside us without becoming too impressed with ourselves, because the part about *us* is no longer the main thing. This is the process of being conformed to the image of Christ. This is also part of our freedom in him. One of the things God sets us free to do in this life is to see ourselves as we truly are—ugly yet in his eyes beautiful—because it is in this state that God loves us so lavishly.

Peter denied knowing Christ, realized what he had done, wept bitterly, and returned to Christ. In contrast, Judas betrayed Christ and stayed away; his heart did not return to Christ. One could argue that this was all predestined, and there would be truth to that. Only God can

judge the hearts of men and women. But as Brennan
Manning points out, God is pleased when we allow that his
compassion is bigger than our sinfulness. When we stubbornly cling to self-rejection, it's like refusing to open our
Christmas presents because we think we don't deserve
them. How would you feel if your child or another loved
one responded that way to your
gift? We are all guilty of denying
Christ in different ways, but he
wants only for us to return to
him and receive his love, no
matter what our crimes have
been.

God is pleased when
we allow that his
compassion is bigger
than our sinfulness.
When we stubbornly
cling to self-
rejection, it's like
refusing to open our
Christmas presents
because we think we
don't deserve them.

It takes Christ's courage to
make us brave enough to look
at the dark places in our hearts
as he shines a light on them.
But there is great reward for
those who do. Sixteenth-century
Spanish mystic Teresa of Avila
said, "If you are willing to
serenely bear the trial of being
displeasing to yourself, then
you will be for Jesus, a pleasant
place of shelter."[9] Others in

your family and community will also benefit from your
willingness to face the truth about yourself; your relationships will be strengthened, and you will be living
with greater integrity.

A glimpse into the compassionate eyes of Christ transforms us, making us what we become, since he thoroughly
knows who we are. When we see Jesus as bigger than anything
about us, the "attitude of the self toward the self," which is
always changing, is overlaid with a transparency of divine
knowledge of the self that is always truth, yet evolves as we
mature. A little girl looks into her daddy's eyes and gains
confidence that she can ride her bike without training wheels
because she remembers the times she's practiced and heard
his words of encouragement, "You can do it," and off she

goes! Years later that same girl prepares to give the valedictory address to her high school classmates, catches the eye of her dad in the audience, sees his wink of confidence, and delivers the speech of a lifetime. Our image of ourselves comes into focus as we look through God's eyes and believe we are the person *he* knows we are. He will make us into the miracles he created us to be.

If you were not fortunate enough to have a parent or other significant person who saw your potential during your growing-up years, there is still hope for living a fulfilling life. You can get fresh glimpses into the eyes of Christ through his Word, through mentors and friends, through intentional repetitions of truthful messages to yourself when things are going well, through reminders to yourself of the One you belong to. These tools can help you find the emotional attunement to God that appears to come naturally and easily to some Christians. As we fix our eyes on Christ, he gradually transforms us into his likeness, one day at a time, just as the sun rises "A Ribbon at a time."[10]

Frederick Buechner calls stories like Paula's and Brennan's "tales of transformation," in which "the ones who live happily ever after . . . are transformed into what they have it in them at their best to be."[11] Like Paula, as a Christian you are a princess of the King of heaven, who has called you to take up your cross, live as the person he knows you are, and follow him to the crest of his Pridelands.

Perhaps you are like Simba. Perhaps you have forgotten who you are, forgotten the redemptive work your Father has done in your heart. Look beyond your interior darkness and see Jesus calling you into the shaft of light beyond all prisons. Arise and walk. Trust that his image is reflected in you somehow, in a way you may not be able to see. Remember the truth.

As you see God, he shows you who you are.

In knowing him moment by moment, you become the miracle he knows you are.

You are a child of God.

Remember.

• • •

"YES, I SWORE AN OATH TO YOU AND
ENTERED INTO A COVENANT WITH YOU,
AND YOU BECAME MINE," SAYS THE LORD GOD.

Ezekiel 16:8, NKJV

RELINQUISHING THE
WAND OF DENIAL

Moving from Magical Thinking to Mindfulness

• • •

WHEN I WAS A CHILD, I TALKED

LIKE A CHILD, I THOUGHT LIKE A CHILD,

I REASONED LIKE A CHILD. WHEN

I BECAME A MAN, I PUT CHILDISH

WAYS BEHIND ME.

1 Corinthians 13:11

Stay back, Meg," my friend Guianna warned her five-year-old granddaughter. Guianna was sweeping up slivers of her broken glass tabletop the morning after a severe Texas windstorm blew it off its base. "I don't want you to get hurt, so you wait for me in the house while I finish cleaning up this mess."

When Guianna finished her sweeping and entered the living room, she found Meg sitting on the couch, head down, arms folded, bottom lip out, not happy. "Meg, what's wrong?" she asked.

"Well!" Meg said, as if insulted. "I asked Jesus to heal your table!"

Can you remember a time when you related to God as a wand-waving worker of miracles as little Meg did? I know I can. The first seminar I ever taught in a church was titled

"Reality Doesn't Bite." The idea behind the seminar was that if Christians followed earnestly after God, he would guarantee that reality wouldn't bite us, at least not too hard. I pictured the Christian life as such a happy tale, a problem-free here and now in which God would somehow sort of magically fix all the yucky circumstances in my life without any need for personal growth or change on my part. And I heard others talking about their faith in the same way.

As time passes, however, the glitter wears off our childish notions that the gospel is a magical tale, and we find our only hope in a true story believed with childlike faith. When we reflect on the years we've spent with God, we have to admit that he hasn't always put our Humpty-Dumpties together again in just the way we'd envisioned. Questions arise, and we may have an emotional wrestling match with God as Jacob, Moses, David, and many others did.

> When we reflect on the years we've spent with God, we have to admit that he hasn't always put our Humpty-Dumpties together again in just the way we'd envisioned.

All the while, our invisible fulfillment (invisible because it's not time for us to see it yet) sits waiting on a different wall from the one we've had our prayer ladder leaned up against. We don't understand the timing. We don't understand the circumstances. It's probably true to say that if we really understood much at all about the power of prayer, we'd lose our nerve altogether. Given that fact, perhaps our days of magical thinking about how God works have their place.

GROWING INTO CHILDLIKE FAITH

• • •

THOSE WHO HAVE ATTAINED CONSIDERABLE
SPIRITUAL STATURE ARE FREQUENTLY
NOTED FOR THEIR 'CHILDLIKENESS.' WHAT THIS

REALLY MEANS IS THAT THEY DO NOT USE

THEIR FACE AND BODY TO HIDE

THEIR SPIRITUAL REALITY.

Dallas Willard[1]

In our attempts to be obedient and grow spiritually mature, many of us remain naïvely *childish* in our faith, approaching God with intense desperation, clutching a list of demands, followed by our vows of loyalty if only he'll follow our directions. Although we may pray with the best of intentions, we see Christ demonstrating a different, *childlike,* dependent trust in the Garden of Gethsemane, when he ended his most desperate prayer with "Yet I want your will, not mine" (Matthew 26:39, NLT). Childlikeness is an ageless quality of transparent vulnerability that keeps us openhandedly dependent on God and grounded in reality. Richard Foster said, "A soul will never grow until it is able to let go of the tight grasp it has on God."[2] We must learn that the white-knuckle approach doesn't work in the spiritual life if we are to move past denial into joyful lives full of God's blessings.

Freelance artist and writer Kathy Doerge found a way to express this in a writing she titled "The Great Exchange":

> I was thinking about what happens when we go through intense times; whether good or bad, we clench our hands. We do this when we are hurt, or scared, or angry, but also if we are really excited. We squeal with delight and clench our hands. But with clenched hands, we cannot receive.
>
> The great exchange is when I open my hands to God and give him my anger, my fear, my sin, my resentment. . . . I give it to him, and he gives me his love, his peace, his forgiveness, his hope. Wow! What a deal. I was talking to him the other day.
>
> "You know, Lord, with this exchange, you're getting a raw deal!"

"Yes, dear child . . . I know very well how raw it is; that is what I suffered and endured on the Cross. But I also get you, and that means the world to me."

The key is unclenching the hands, and that comes as we honestly acknowledge our pain, our fear, our confusion, our disappointment, our frailty (and sometimes we need someone to help us with that). But then with open hands we can receive all he has for us.[3]

• • •

I CALL TO YOU, O LORD, EVERY DAY;

I SPREAD OUT MY HANDS TO YOU.

Psalm 88:9

To live mindfully is to face with childlike integrity the condition of our souls in the moment and to call on God for strength and grace to see what is real in our lives instead of disowning what we wish were not true. It is being aware of our spiritual reality instead of hiding from it. It takes more faith to listen to God prayerfully and to honestly name our needs to him and be still than it does to believe in any guaranteed outcome that favors our terms.

We can apply mindfulness to many facets of life, but in this chapter we will address the maturing process of the soul through increased self-awareness as God reveals it to us. At times we may need to gain some life experience before we can face reality, and this is as God would have it. When my hus-

To live mindfully is to face with childlike integrity the condition of our souls in the moment and to call on God for strength and grace to see what is real in our lives instead of disowning what we wish were not true. It is being aware of our spiritual reality instead of hiding from it.

band, Frank, was nine years old, his mother became ill. She was required to rest in bed, and a doctor friend came often to examine her. Frank and his two sisters, Karen and Marget, knew nothing of the illness their Swedish-born mother, thirty-eight-year-old Siev Waggoner, bore as she managed to smile and suffer quietly from severe headaches of an unknown cause. One day the three children went out with a friend, and when they returned and ran to the bedroom to greet their mom, she was gone.

Soon Frank's dad took the three children to the hospital, and shortly thereafter they were told their mother had died. Although they could not fully comprehend the meaning of words like *aneurysm* or realize the lifelong impact of *death,* they began to cry. They did know that the mother who had read them stories, clipped their toenails, taught them to pray and brush their teeth was not there. They all felt unbearably sad. The oldest sister, Karen, gathered her two younger siblings together to try to comfort them, patting their little backs. A few days later at the funeral, the children stood bravely beside their father as the cloying sound of the organ played in the background and friends filed past the casket.

A short while later Frank's dad remarried, and the family moved from their home in bustling Kansas City to the Rio Hondo Valley of Texas, where banana trees grew in the schoolyard. Here in their new home, they met new friends at school and church. The new Mrs. Waggoner was introduced to everyone as the children's mother; the family acted as if everything was normal, and life went on. As time passed, Frank began to spend countless hours alone in his bedroom, tinkering with old engines, taking mechanical things apart and putting them back together. This coping mechanism of distraction kept his mind off the pain of his mother's mysterious death, and Frank had no awareness of the unresolved grief that lay buried deep within his heart.

One evening years later Frank and I were watching the movie *Shadowlands.* When we got to the part when C. S. Lewis's wife, Joy, dies of cancer and Lewis sits down on the stairs to comfort her son, Douglas, unexpected tears brimmed in Frank's eyes as he heard Lewis's words to Douglas: "My mother died when I was nine years old." These words triggered the grief Frank had never talked about or thoroughly expressed. At last he was able to release the pent-up tears of a hurting child's heart inside a rugged man's body. "There is a time for everything, and a season for every activity under heaven," said King Solomon in Ecclesiastes 3:1. Frank's deep pain had lain buried within his heart until later when it was time to face it.

COMING OUT OF HIDING

• • •

SEARCH ME, O GOD, AND KNOW MY HEART;

TEST ME AND KNOW MY ANXIOUS THOUGHTS.

Psalm 139:23

Sometimes when we repress grief, it is God's way of helping us survive or strengthening us until we're ready to face reality because we have become more aware of ourselves as well as more aware of the truths of God. I recall a time as a graduate student in a psychology class when I naively declared, "I don't care about becoming self-aware; I only want to be God-aware," not realizing they go hand in hand. If denial were not so powerful and deceptive, we wouldn't be so easily tricked into doing things we don't really want to do, such as getting tangled up in addictions, unhealthy relationships, and all kinds of things that distract us from the heart of God. The problem is, temptation comes in subtle ways, not obvious ones.

At a national conference of Christian counselors, Dr. Keith Miller, author of *The Secret Life of the Soul* and many other books, vulnerably told his colleagues how his successful career had spiraled out of control and ended in an extramarital affair when he unwittingly became more devoted to the ministry than to God: "I saw that inside our lives, where we seldom take other people, there is a secret life of the soul, an intimate adventure that can reveal or hide much of the baffling glory and tragedy of one's life—even from one's self."[4]

God always knew we would struggle with facing the truth about ourselves and our lives; in fact, he's set it up so that we can't mature in our spiritual lives without him. As Christians we sometimes like to skip over the step of recognizing the problem for what it really is (denial of what is true about us) and call that "faith." But unless we get reality into focus—learn to call sin sin, and pain pain—sooner or later we may get caught in a fog of unreality.

Often a crisis serves as a catalyst for drawing us out of our emotional hiding places. "Sometimes we simply don't want to face the truth about ourselves, the myth reads so much better," says Sheila Walsh, former cohost of television's 700 Club. Sheila checked herself into a psychiatric hospital when inner turmoil plagued her to the point where she could no longer cope.

In her book Honestly, Sheila says, "Sometimes I think we misinterpret faith. In my own life, instead of grabbing hold of what was wrong with it and dealing with it, no matter how painful it was, I acted as if everything were fine. I thought if I just believed enough, then everything would be all right. But was I living by faith or by wishful thinking?"[5] How would you respond to Sheila's question? Has there been a time in your life when you tried to believe hard enough so that something you hoped for would come true? This can be confusing. God can and does work miracles, but he does so at his own bidding and not according to our instructions and timetable. He is God.

Joni Eareckson Tada explains in the foreword to Sheila's book how shocked she was to hear the news that Sheila Walsh, a strong, talented, charismatic television personality, had committed herself for inpatient psychiatric care. It was so contrary to her public image. Yet when Sheila came to speak to Joni's office staff after she'd finished her rehab, it was a different woman who stood before the group. She appeared much more gentle, tender, broken. Sheila still had the power and clarity she always had, but it was obviously Christ's strength showing through Sheila's weakness as she spoke in a straightforward and dynamic way about "a God who lives near the floor." This was the gracious God she encountered in the hospital, the God who loved her just as she was, fears, anxieties, and all, and who invited her to share her spiritual reality instead of hiding it, to grow out of childish thinking and into childlike faith.

Sheila challenges the church to become a place where we can talk about how things really are. "In our desire to be an inspiration to one another we often veil what is true, because what is true is not always inspirational. But hurting believers whose lives are in tatters often need real help. If we were able to put aside our need for approval long enough to be authentic, then, surely, we would be living as the church."[6]

In our desire to be an inspiration to one another we often veil what is true, because what is true is not always inspirational. But hurting believers whose lives are in tatters often need real help. If we were able to put aside our need for approval long enough to be authentic, then, surely, we would be living as the church.

—Sheila Walsh,
Honestly

One Sunday morning a group of good friends engaged in a stimulating Sunday school class discussion. I don't recall the exact topic, but it had to do with the paradoxical nature of some biblical truths—whoever wishes to save his life shall lose it; the first will be last; in giving we receive—those seemingly opposing truths we sometimes wrestle with as we try to follow God's ways. Suddenly one of our deep thinkers I'll call Tony took a risk as he vulnerably interjected, "Why does God have to be so schizophrenic?" A shocked silence filled the room.

An honest exchange of ideas might have been quite helpful to Tony as he tried to align some of the current circumstances of his personal life with biblical truth. An open forum could have helped him connect with others who'd faced similar dilemmas.

Our wizened instructor, an endearing elderly man, scratched his white beard and looked around to see if anyone would respond. People began shifting their weight uneasily, shuffling through their Bibles to fill the uncomfortable space of time. I wondered if someone would stand and shout, "Blasphemer!" Finally the silence grew so uncomfortable that someone awkwardly switched the subject to something safer, and Tony was left alone with his mind-boggling ponderings.

At some point, if our faith is to become our own, we will all search for sanity and wisdom in the midst of biblical paradox, coming to understand that we, as well as God, are not schizophrenic, and yet "split realities" do exist. *If God loves me, why did he let my child die? If God is always with me, why do I feel so alone? How can God be all-knowing and allow my daughter to be sexually abused?* Although we seldom find answers, voicing our questions can help us maintain integrity and congruence as we face reality.

One of the reasons that support groups based on a twelve-step program are so effective in ministry is that they *affirm* people for telling the truth about themselves and confronting reality instead of hiding it. People are not left alone to do their grieving or to hide in shame because they don't look strong. Instead, they receive love and acceptance just as they are, in their imperfect, human condition. Without supportive friends who will remind us of truth when we're struggling, we can get bogged down in feelings, overwhelmed with reality, and become increasingly isolated and confused.

Once I facilitated a small support group for women (there were only three members, all wives of laypastors). Over time these women began to let down their spiritual hair, vent their frustrations, and pray transparently for one another. One week they compiled a list of Scripture texts showing how the saints of old cried out to God from their hearts, lamenting as often as they praised, wrestling with God as part of their intimate life with him in the midst of their realities. The women began to move from denial about their struggles to acceptance of themselves as human beings in need of God, encouraging each other as they discovered that they were not alone in their difficulties.

"I didn't want to admit how resentful I am about the demands of the ministry," Sarah said. "I felt so guilty because I did not feel loving toward the women in our church. But listen to what Moses said to God in Numbers 11: 'I cannot carry all these people by myself; the burden is too heavy for me. If this is how you are going to treat me, put me to death right now—if I have found favor in your eyes—and do not let me face my own ruin.'"

Somehow Moses' honest complaint gave Sarah permission to be genuine with God in her own prayers. With fresh insight, Sarah explained how this helped her.

"First I named my problem by admitting my resentment that people expect so much of me and I get so little appreciation."

"I can relate to that," Barbara said. "I often feel sorry for myself because I have no time to do anything I enjoy, but I don't dare admit it to anyone, not even my husband."

"Oh, but that's the best part!" Sarah continued. "Admitting my resentment helped me uncover a deeper discovery: my own hidden demand that people treat me as if I were special. Suddenly I realized that God was prompting me to accept myself as a limited human being because that's all I am. I needed God to remove my pride and give me faith that I could do all he calls me to do." Sarah had ended her soul-searching prayer time with praise for God's sufficiency and a deeper awareness of his sovereignty. The other women in the group were encouraged that they, too, could honestly express their needs to God and then wait, casting their anxieties at the feet of Christ and leaving them there. They didn't feel compelled to inspire one another; it was enough to trust God together.

Ironically, the women found mutual inspiration without even trying. They discovered that their emotional loads were considerably lighter, and they became more loving toward one another, more aware of God as our truly Wonderful Counselor—a God who prefers integrity over perfection, vulnerability among fellow Christians over the ability to inspire others. These pastors' wives had missed these important insights as long as they felt compelled always to be strong and have the answers for everyone in their congregations. I admired these women greatly and often smiled to myself as I reflected on the insights they were passing on to the women who looked to them for leadership.

GRACE BEYOND REALITY

• • •

THE SWEET SOUND OF AMAZING GRACE
SAVES US FROM THE NECESSITY OF SELF-DECEPTION.
IT KEEPS US FROM DENYING THAT THOUGH
CHRIST WAS VICTORIOUS, THE BATTLE
WITH LUST, GREED, AND PRIDE
STILL RAGES WITHIN US.

Brennan Manning[7]

When you dare to open yourself to truthfulness, as was the case with Pandora's box, you're never quite sure what all may fly in your face. None of us could face all the ugliness and weakness in ourselves all at once, so God in his mercy reveals it to us a little at a time. We needn't go probing into the darkness of our unconscious, pressure ourselves to "figure out" things we don't yet understand, or rush the healing process. It's enough to face the truth as God brings it into the light.

My two sons are adults now. After some time and distance from the days of our family breakup, I was able to look back on my behavior as a young Christian mom less defensively, admit some of my contributions to the breakup of my first marriage, and discuss it with my sons at appropriate times. During the first five years of that marriage (before I became a Christian), my husband and I argued quite often; occasionally we'd have a blowup and then continue on. But once I started to try to base my life on biblical principles, I determined to hold back any strongly confrontive responses and instead give a soft answer in hopes of turning away wrath.

Even when my husband started staying away from home long hours after work, I thought if I just prayed long enough and hard enough, God would change his heart. Instead of getting professional help or telling friends and family of our troubled private life, we grew further apart emotionally. We no longer talked honestly or touched each other with tenderness. He avoided intimacy by staying away from home while I was frozen in fear of what reality might hold if I dared to face it.

I had misunderstood what the Bible taught, of course, and had bought into the fallacy that "good Christians (especially women) don't get angry," mistakenly believing that I was not mad if I didn't yell at my husband or retaliate. During those pre–*Love Must Be Tough* days I hadn't heard anyone talk about the need for Christian women to ask for respect in relationships or define ways to protect themselves or their children from emotional and verbal abuse. Biblical phrases such as "My strength is made perfect in weakness" (2 Corinthians 12:9, NKJV) seemed to mean that being nonassertive, enabling, and weak willed was somehow godly. (I didn't know it at the time, but this is quite the opposite of what we see in the life of the apostle Paul, who was strong willed *for God* and weak only in that he did not get his way with the world, which eventually resulted in his death.) In self-righteous attempts to avoid "thinking too highly of myself," I denied my own needs.

I had fallen into a twisted, Christianized version of "learned helplessness," becoming a religious Stepford Wife who operated from a panel of control buttons programmed to try to hold a marriage together instead of living in God's strength from my heart. Where had all my feelings gone? What had happened to my desires, my longings, my once-cherished love of childlike play and lighthearted fun? Studying the Bible, praying, and going to church are good disciplines to practice, and I did them with regularity—calculated regularity. But God later began to show me how I'd done so much of it legalistically and for the wrong reasons—not to please him but to control the outcome of my marriage. Terrified of failure, I became a hollow perfectionist at the "good Christian wife" role.

When my first husband left home and filed for divorce, I was devastated to learn he'd been unfaithful. At last I was forced to admit my failure and imperfection, and I finally sought help from a Christian counselor who exposed my denial. Scott and Brent had prayed that God would bring Daddy back home, but he didn't come back. A mysterious silence accompanied Daddy's absence because Mommy didn't know how to explain. Doubts and fears and questions about God's character were buried in my sons' young hearts, waiting to resurface at a later time when they (and their mommy) were more mature. In all my self-focused efforts to live biblically, I'd entirely missed the point of the gospel—the love of God for sinners such as myself—and in so doing, my two sons became quite confused about the character of God.

Years later I would begin to talk with my sons about the realities of their childhood and our God—a God who refuses to be bargained with or take his direction from us but asks that we trust his infinitely compassionate heart. As I looked back through timeworn eyes, I could see my self-righteousness during my years as a young mom, when I talked and thought as a spiritual child, and some of the ways this affected my sons' lives. We discussed anger and how their dad expressed his by acting out while I turned mine inward and became depressed. Talking about these things helped my sons become aware of their personal anger styles, their hurts and fears, and their reluctance to take risks. It also helped them to clarify their responsibility for choices they make as adults.

Sometimes reality bites hard. God's children are not exempt. But scars and stains from this life cannot transcend the reality of God's grace. Admitting my imperfections to my sons helped us all heal a little so we could become good friends. I find them gracious and forgiving, seemingly intuitive of my good intentions back in the days of my "magical thinking," and affirming toward me for the spiritual disciplines they saw me practice and the exposure to Christian values they received in our home.

God *is* a worker of divine miracles, but this life is not a magic show he puts on for our entertainment. We are holy people because we belong to God, and for no other reason. These days of the Meantime, falling between our taking Christ as Savior and meeting him face-to-face in heaven, are strewn with searching, strife, and joy. We enter into authentic faith when we offer to God our fears and doubts as well as our praise and gratitude. In *A Place for You* Paul Tournier describes the experience of being "in between"—between the time we leave home and arrive at our destination; between the time we leave adolescence and arrive at adulthood; between the time we leave doubt and arrive at faith: "When the environment of our lives changes . . . we find ourselves in a 'middle of the way' between the ideas and customs of the past, and the ideas and customs of the future, and this situation is charged with anxiety. Moreover, the whole of life may be looked upon as a 'middle of the way' . . . between the maternal bosom and that of God. In between there is necessarily anxiety."[8]

As we are mindful of God's presence with us, seeing him as the solution beyond any problems we have and trusting our Wonderful Counselor to accept us with all our feelings and imperfections, we will be strong enough to bear reality one day at a time. We will even find freedom and joy in the midst of life's cruel realities. As God teaches and enables us, our weakness turns into strength, and our fear is transformed into courage.

Five-year-old Andrew, the grandson of a friend of mine, needed a vaccination. As is true of most people at any age when they're about to get a shot, he was afraid. On the way to the doctor's office, Andrew started to whine, and his mother said, "Now, Andrew, you know you have to get the shot so you can stay well. The nurse knows it will sting a little bit, and it's hard for her to give it to you because she doesn't like to hurt people." (I imagine little Andrew might have been disappointed to learn he could not escape the horror to come.) "You can either pout and whine and cry about it, or you can be brave and grateful to get a shot that will help you be well. It's your choice."

By the time they got to the doctor's office and the nurse came in with the needle, Andrew smiled quietly and closed his eyes. After the injection he looked up and said, "Thank you for the shot, Miss Nurse! I know it was hard for you to do because you don't like to hurt people. But you did it because it will help me, so I wanted to say thank you for the shot!"

Andrew gained courage to face a difficult reality by transparently admitting his fear and looking past the problem to see something good. He was mindful of the benefits of staying well, and he was grateful for the nurse's help. Like Andrew, we can be mindful of ways God is setting our perspectives straight, grateful for the courage to look reality in the eye. We can name our fears and trust God to turn them into courage. We can unclench our fists and give him our burdens.

Be mindful of the joys all around you. God has sprinkled them over all the earth. Children are laughing somewhere at this very moment—can you hear them? Little old ladies are smiling contented smiles. Flowers are blooming or leaves are changing color or snow is falling gently. Celebrations are waiting to happen. Chocolate cakes and crème brûlées are waiting to be savored. Which little joys and delights are you aware of in this very moment?

• • •

YOU'RE BLESSED WHEN YOU GET YOUR
INSIDE WORLD—YOUR MIND AND HEART—
PUT RIGHT. THEN YOU CAN SEE GOD
IN THE OUTSIDE WORLD.

Matthew 5:8, *THE MESSAGE*

WIELDING THE SHIELD OF SELF-PROTECTION

Surrendering Control in Strength, Not Weakness

• • •

THE LORD OF THE CASTLE MUST HAVE

THE POWER TO DECIDE WHEN TO DRAW

THE BRIDGE AND WHEN TO LET IT DOWN. . . .

IT IS IMPORTANT FOR YOU TO CONTROL

YOUR OWN DRAWBRIDGE.

Henri Nouwen[1]

One day as I was doing some after-Christmas unshopping at Wal-Mart, a profound insight dawned on me. It came as I watched two preschoolers and their young mother waiting in the checkout line in front of me.

"Mine!" a pudgy, sullen-faced little girl said, yanking a Tiny Tots makeup kit from her big sister's hand.

"I'm just looking at it!" came the angry sibling's response. "Don't be so selfish!"

"No! Mine!" shouted the little sister, now stomping her foot and beginning to cry.

"Sarah!" yelled the young mom, bending down to toddler height. "You know you're supposed to share nicely. Now let your sister see your new toy, or I won't buy it for you!"

From an early age our parents teach us to share what's given to us, to be nice, to be generous, or else we'll be labeled selfish. Added to our parents' reminders about sharing, the Bible instructs us to consider the needs of others more important than our own, to love each other even as Christ himself has loved us. Occasionally we witness one of those rare times when God calls people to really lay down their lives for another, as Dr. Robertson McQuilkin did when he quit his job as president of Columbia Bible College to take care of his wife, Muriel, when she fell victim to Alzheimer's. In his tender tale told in *A Promise Kept,* Dr. McQuilkin writes of tending Muriel, cleaning up her messes, searching for her in panicky pursuit when she wandered away from home, and his decision to care for her full-time because Muriel felt more secure with him around.[2]

> With regret we may realize we've tried to be selfless when God wasn't in it—we've succumbed to the pressure from people instead of saving our energy and time for the mission God has planned for us.

Dr. McQuilkin took care of his wife not merely out of duty but because he loved her. We are awed when we observe the peaceful grace of a life surrendered to God, the love of Christ personified, and we sincerely hope we would be up to the task of proving our devotion to God and others when we're called upon. When God calls us to such a task, he supplies the strength and grace to accomplish it and delights in being the source of our power. But if we don't have some clarity on who's assigning the task and supplying the energy, we may get ourselves into trouble.

We know God created us for good works but for *which* good works? We're vulnerable to accepting a "mission impossible" out of guilt (who will do it if I don't?). The project begins to feel like a burden. We may grow tired, angry, resentful, and then scratch our heads and wonder what we did wrong. And that's a far cry from Dr.

McQuilkin's words about his wife: "I love to care for her. She's my precious."[3] With regret we may realize we've tried to be selfless when God wasn't in it—we've succumbed to the pressure from people instead of saving our energy and time for the mission God has planned for us.

Even though God is the all-powerful Creator of the universe, when it comes to having his way in our lives, he doesn't stomp his foot and selfishly demand "Mine!" like the little girl at Wal-Mart. Instead of wielding his power to force us to obey him, he woos us, invites us to join our hearts, minds, and souls with his before all others. God has given us the gift of free will, and he prefers that we *choose* to trust him moment by moment because demanding our way never leads to true contentment and peace. Transitioning from *mine* to *his* may sound easy, like something that happens as instantly as closing the door to our childhood home behind us. But it's more likely to take a lifetime as we become attuned to his still, quiet voice beckoning us to respond and to trust the safety of our heavenly Father's steadfast guiding hand.

WILL YOU?

• • •

REST, REST, REST IN GOD'S LOVE.
THE ONLY WORK YOU ARE REQUIRED
NOW TO DO IS TO GIVE YOUR MOST
INTENSE ATTENTION TO HIS STILL,
SMALL VOICE WITHIN.

Madame Jeanne Guyon[4]

Sometimes during the course of our growing up, our trust and safety instincts become injured. Whether through unintentional mistreatment by one of our caregivers, neglect, or some other form of human imperfection, our child-of-God instincts were thwarted, and we learned to cast them aside in favor of what those in power said we should do. Of course, it's a good thing to avoid friction when we obey those in authority over us. But sometimes we carry that too far. By learning to mistrust our own flawed judgment, we feel guilty when we consider our own needs, even when we may be thirty or forty or fifty years old. When that happens, we may confuse the voices of people who have their own plans for how we should spend our time and energy with God's holy whisper inside us. Sometimes it takes practice to listen for God as he gains (or regains) our trust, so that he is the One directing the course of our lives. We may also need to work on understanding the connection between safety, trust, and our own instincts.

In *The Man Who Listens to Horses,* Monty Roberts describes a way to train horses by gaining their instinctual trust instead of by beating them into submission. Monty grew up on a ranch with his father, who broke horses the traditional way through the use of dominance, exhaustion, and whippings. Since Monty's father had also beaten him, sometimes with whips and chains, he thought as he watched his father work with the horses that surely there must be a better way to get a horse to accept a rider.

So he started observing the animals, how they related to each other, and especially the dominant mare in the group. He studied her timing when she cocked her ear, lowered her head, and turned her body slightly, inviting a horse to come back in with the group. He called this behavior "join up." Monty found greater success in training horses by gaining their trust, by asking them, "Will you?" than traditional trainers who demanded, "You must."[5]

As Christian women we hear our strong and gentle Lord daily whisper inside our hearts, asking, *Will you? Will you do it my way today?* As our supreme authority he *could* force us, but instead he calls to us and waits for our response. He wants us to become loving people, obedient to his way because it works. Steve Brown, author and president of Key Life Ministries, says, "The law reflects the parameters of God's desire—not the parameters of his love."[6] Because God loves us, he wants us to follow his guidelines and not be harmed by our poor choices. Yet he leaves the options open to us. If he had not given us the privilege of making our own choices, we would not really be free to be his.

"If we were forced to love Jesus and to respond to him only as he ordered, we would not really be lovers," writes Henry Nouwen.[7] It sounds so simple to just "trust and obey." We may very sincerely want to obey the commandments Jesus said were the most important: "Love the Lord your God with all your heart and with all your soul and with all your mind and with all your strength" and "Love your neighbor as yourself" (Mark 12:30-31). The rub comes when we try to live this out in our everyday lives, in our relationships with others.

No Other Gods before Him

• • •

WE MUST RELINQUISH CONTROL, MUST HOLD
WITH AN OPEN HAND ALL THOSE
RELATIONSHIPS AND ACTIVITIES AND
POSSESSIONS GOD HAS SO GRACIOUSLY GIVEN
US, BUT THAT WE ARE SORELY TEMPTED TO
CLING TO AS SUBSTITUTES FOR GOD HIMSELF.

E. Stanley Jones[8]

Kara had served almost seven years as women's ministry coordinator in the large church she attended. After praying considerably for God's direction, she announced to Valerie, the pastor's wife, that she would soon step down from the leadership position. In anticipation of this welcome respite Kara now looked forward to spending time with her six-month-old grandson. She had also recently developed some health problems, and her doctor's advice only affirmed her plans to slow down.

What was unknown to Kara at the time was that Valerie had planned to depart soon on a month-long mission trip in Russia. The news of Kara's resignation was both untimely and unsettling since it meant the women's ministry duties would fall to Valerie if a volunteer to replace Kara didn't present herself quickly.

"What will the women do without you?" Valerie queried in an agitated tone, and then she broke the news to Kara about her own plans to be away. "Have you considered serving just one more year?" Kara's spirit wilted as Valerie continued. "Can you honestly say you've prayed about this for a period of time?"

As Kara recounted this story to me, she reviewed her collection of fond memories during her years of service in church leadership. "I've loved getting women involved, drawing them out, encouraging them to use their talents to reach out to others. I think my favorite project of all was the monthly community dinners. At least a dozen of us would pitch in to help, giving out bowls of homemade turkey and vegetable soup to anyone in this neighborhood who needed a free dinner," Kara said wistfully. "It's been a lot of work, but the fulfillment for me comes in seeing the joy in faces of people, both givers and receivers. So many folks in the community have come to know about God and his love through those bowls of soup."

Kara paused pensively, as if sorting her scattered memories into stacks of reasons to remain in her leadership position versus reasons to resign. "But lately, I really have strongly sensed God urging me to slow down my usual breakneck pace. I sense that for several reasons, my health included, it's time to pass the leadership baton. Still, Valerie's words echo in my mind, and I truly want to be obedient to God. I certainly don't want her to miss the mission trip because of me. Am I really just being selfish?"

Kara's question is one I often hear from women, and one I experienced personally in my encounter with the legalistic pastor (in chapter 2). Christians are especially susceptible to becoming overresponsible and overgiving, sometimes detrimentally disregarding their own needs and even abandoning good personal health care. It seems so Christian, so right, to put others' needs ahead of our own. We may not see the need to keep our lives from becoming overly entangled with others so that we are free to yield to God. Yet if we give away all we have to serve in our churches, we may find our inner lives depleted, our families neglected, and ourselves confused about why our behavior is not glorifying God as we hoped it would.

There are many good books that can help people to develop healthy boundaries in their relationships and to respect the choices and changes of other adults they love. I think of codependency as an invasion of the holy space inside each person that should be reserved for God alone. As we guard that inner sanctum for him first, other priorities in our marriages, our friendships, our churches, and other circles of influence fall gracefully into place. Only when we have this priority in order do we have anything of eternal value to give to those other "good things," and then it is from God's heart that we give, not just from our own, although our humanness is always part of the mix. We are not the savior; Christ is. He has not called us to pay the price of saving the world; he has already done that.

Remember the concept of the "God-shaped vacuum" that only he can fill? When I first heard this term, I thought it applied only to salvation. I believed that once people invited Christ to live inside them, the vacuum was filled. Of course, this is true. But later I also came to see this holy space as Christ's exclusive living quarters for the duration of our lives. It is the place where the true self meets with the Holy Spirit, where we find peace and rest, where we can check with him for direction. It is the place where we are most sure we are "his."

Other people also have this holy inner space in which God speaks to them. Each day we go out into the world and encounter the joys and pains of our community, always returning to our own lives—the gift he has given us to live fully—in the present moment, aware of his love. With deep compassion for the needy and hurting, we pray, do what we can, and rest in God. We may give our opinion or advice, but we must also take care not to stomp on others' divine inner space by demanding, "You must do it my way." Instead, we need to encourage others to listen for God's voice within, ask them to do it his way. This way of relating to people encourages mutual respect and ultimate trust in God and suggests that we find protection for ourselves and for others through mutual surrender to him. It requires that we hone our listening skills, pray fervently for one another, and realize that *we* may not know the right answer but God does.

If you surrender yourself to God's way, declare yourself "His," you cannot also surrender yourself with equal dedication to other people. God alone is holy. If you desire to put his glory above people's approval and so sometimes say no when others want you to say yes because it fits their agenda, they will sometimes misunderstand and criticize you. In your best attempts to serve God, you may be called selfish, even by your well-meaning Christian brothers and sisters who quote chapter and verse to try to convince you of their view.

When Kara determined to change her priorities, there was a bit of a power struggle over her decision. The tug-of-war was partly with Valerie, because she wanted things done her way, but it was mostly with that part of Kara herself that so desperately needed approval. A control struggle always pulls both ways—it takes two to make it an issue. If I hold securely to my responsibility to answer to God for my life and refuse to fight anybody about it, there won't be any meaningless battle. When conflict does arise and we hold on to our commitment to follow God's way but someone else doesn't agree, God will take care of us. Likewise, if I yank on what's yours and you put your end of the rope down, the game's over.

These power battles can also go on in our relationships with God. They may sound something like this: *Please bless me, dear Lord. I know you can do it. I've been spelling it out to you as clearly as I know how, and you're still not getting it.* Uh-oh! Now we've flip-flopped from our surrender stance to one in which we try to be the burden bearer ourselves, straining to figure things out and make it all work as if *we* must *be* God.

The Scriptures tell us that from the age of twelve Jesus

was about his father's business, growing in wisdom and stature, keeping God's priorities his highest aim, yet not without human feelings and vulnerabilities (see Luke 2:52). As he grows older, we see him consistently holding to this pattern, sometimes pushing out in a boat, away from the crowds who clamored for him, because he needed time to pray or rest. His was a life totally surrendered—heart, mind, and soul—to the guidance of his Father in heaven. Even when his dear friends called for his help, their needs were secondary to God's direction.

Jesus' life was totally surrendered—heart, mind, and soul—to the guidance of his Father in heaven. Even when his dear friends called for his help, their needs were secondary to God's direction.

We see this in chapter 11 of the Gospel of John. When Jesus' friend Lazarus becomes ill, Lazarus's sisters, Mary and Martha, send for Jesus, hoping he will come right away and heal their brother. But when Jesus gets their message, he stays where he is for two more days. Then he and his disciples return to Judea, arriving four days after Lazarus's death. Many friends are visiting Mary and Martha, sympathizing with them over the loss of their brother. When Martha hears that Jesus is coming, she goes out to meet him, saying, "Lord, . . . if you had been here, my brother would not have died" (v. 21). Then Mary comes and falls at Jesus' feet, saying the exact same words: "Lord, if you had been here, my brother would not have died" (v. 32).

Mary and Martha's "if onlys" have a familiar ring and even bear some similarity to Valerie's criticism of Kara's resignation. Being one with God, Jesus was finely attuned to his Father's will. He was very clear about what God was asking and was not the least bit threatened when good friends didn't see things his way. "It is for God's glory so that God's Son may be glorified through it," he had said before returning to Judea to raise Lazarus, who was already dead.

When God was making his covenant with Abram in Genesis 15:1, Abram did not see how God could make him a father of many since he had no worthy heir. But God came to him in a vision and said, "Do not be afraid, Abram. I am your shield, your very great reward." As Abram's king, God was both his protector and his reward. As you go about your everyday life, how do you stay aware that you are shielded by God's kingship? The Scriptures say that he is our shield, but how does that play out in us from day to day?

Kara became confused because someone she admired was telling her, "You must do it my way." She had learned not to trust her own instincts, to value the opinions of those she looked up to, even to the point of ignoring her own. God created us for his purposes, for his kingdom's glory, not for others' agendas. Once Kara drew away to herself to listen, to discover what God was saying to her, her heart quieted. She reviewed her reasoning and the direction she believed God had given to her: to care for her health, to spend time with her grandchild, to do what he wanted her to do with her life. In that still place in her soul, God reassured Kara that he was in control and that her decision was "His."

CHOOSING TO BE HIS

• • •

PRAYER IS THE PLACE WHERE WE
SORT OUT OUR DESIRES AND WHERE
WE ARE OURSELVES SORTED OUT BY THE
DESIRES WE CHOOSE TO FOLLOW.

Ann and Barry Ulanov[9]

There are many ways in which we can be deceived and lose track of that still, quiet place inside us when loud voices vie for our attention. Even those who have lived long years with God wrestle with the temptation to wield more than their share of power and control. I love the way J. R. R. Tolkien depicts this subtle allure of evil in *The Lord of the*

Rings. Even Gandalf, the elder wizard, is not immune to the temptation to reach for the ring that would give him untold powers. In our lives we will all face different temptations, and they are usually most deceptive when they are aimed at our areas of greatest vulnerability.

Diane had been in my office twice. For about two years she and her husband had grown further and further apart; he worked on home projects in his spare time, and she worked overtime at the office. There was no major conflict or abuse, and their marriage had once been alive and well. But over time their separate lives had led them down two different paths, both destined for isolation, resentment, and indifference.

"I know it's not right," Diane said. "And don't talk to me about God or the Bible; I'm a Christian, and I know all that. It's just that I'm finding myself sexually tempted with a guy at work." As Diane paused, I caught a glimpse of her inner predicament. Her black-and-white world held out only two options to choose from: a dead marriage or an exciting sexual experience—that was all she could see. "It feels so good to be desired and attended to, and I think I'm falling in love. Besides, I've been praying for someone to confide in, and maybe Jim is God's answer to my prayer."

In her naïveté Diane was not aware of her double-bind belief: it wouldn't be right to have an affair with Jim/Jim is God's answer to my prayer. Both could not be true. After we briefly discussed this, I asked about her immediate plans with Jim. Diane had temporarily slammed the door to that inner chamber inside her where the Holy Spirit lived. And today she wasn't particularly interested in what he had to say anyway. My task, as I saw it, was to help comb the tangles from her view of her options so that she had a chance to make a choice. If she didn't assert a firm *no* to the lure of infidelity, a decision would very soon be made for her by default.

Jim had asked Diane to meet him for dinner later that evening, and she wanted to go, but she also recognized her affinity for escape behaviors, avoiding conflict, and wanting intimacy without any real effort.

"So, what choice are you going to make, Diane?" I asked. "Do you really want to have an affair?"

Diane dodged my question and explained how badly she needed attention, to feel that she belonged to someone. She'd come to feel that her husband was rejecting her. She had tried hard to be attractive to him, to be loving, yet he didn't seem to notice. In her attempts to be agreeable and make him happy, she had even quit going anywhere with her women friends because he objected.

Diane had worked full-time for several years and had turned over her paycheck to her husband without any awareness of how he was spending their money because he paid the bills and took care of their investments. Whenever he wanted a new power tool or the latest video equipment, he bought it. Yet when Diane needed shopping money, her husband often told her they were broke. Months had passed without any dates or shared fun times.

In her earlier attempts to love her husband well, Diane had gone too far. She had given much more than she should have, and as a result she had contaminated her inner space where only Christ belonged. She had surrendered the personal power God had given her—which God never asks us to do—and her husband probably didn't know what to do with that or how to respond. It must have been a heavy load. She'd given up asserting her opinions to ensure that she wasn't domineering or bossy to him, and she had rescued her husband instead of holding to a standard of integrity and fairness. These were *her* issues, not her husband's.

After Diane had built her case for having an affair, I wanted to draw her attention to the larger battle going on, one that would recur in a subsequent relationship if she didn't recognize it now. It was a battle over control. Who would hold the power in her life? Would she expect someone else to make her happy? (I don't mean to imply that others' affection doesn't contribute to our happiness, but ultimately contentment and joy are inner qualities.) Would she selfishly declare, "Mine!" and get what she wanted for that moment but ultimately give away her

God-given power in order to experience instant pleasure? Or would she hold on to her gift from God—free will, the freedom to choose—with all its rights and responsibilities?

"Why not claim a life for Diane?" I suggested. As her therapist I hoped to sound an alarm, to get her attention and help Diane see her choices with clarity. I saw both a need to intervene in her urgent, immediate dilemma and also a need to help her look beyond today's circumstances and address her disillusionment with her life. She needed to be taught to fish so that she would have a trade to live by, but in that other choice, the one toward which she was drawn, a few bites of a fresh-caught line trout would offer some immediate gratification and temporarily stave off her soul's starvation for affection and a sense of belonging.

Diane stared at me, puzzled.

"Why not shift your focus from what you *don't* have with your husband to what you *do* have as a woman?" I continued, suggesting she make a firm commitment to her own personal growth and integrity by finding fulfillment through some of her interests in natural history museums, photography, and activities with her female friends. I knew Diane hadn't come to me for a lecture or for marriage counseling. She was looking for a reason to stay true to herself, and ultimately to God, or else she would have been with Jim instead of me, perhaps at that very moment. I hoped she would give herself some time to listen to what her life was telling her.

"I guess I hadn't thought about my life in that way," Diane replied with a tone of uncertainty. "I do want to live with integrity, but I also have needs." I agreed. Before she left my office that day, she had dissolved into tears as the wall of emotional coldness she had built began to melt away. She grieved the loss of intimacy she once shared with her husband. She wept over her empty marriage and her empty self and asked me to pray that she would find the courage to "choose life," not knowing at that moment what would become of her marriage.

That day Diane would have found help from the words of Henri Nouwen in his book *The Inner Voice of Love:* "The great task is to claim yourself for yourself, so that you can contain your needs within the boundaries of your self and hold them in the presence of those you love. True mutuality in love requires people who possess themselves and who can give to each other while holding on to their own identities. So, in order both to give more effectively and to be more self-contained with your needs, you must learn to set boundaries to your love."[10]

I did pray for Diane as she had asked, and prayer is powerful. But I also recognized that the real turning point in our session came when she reconnected with God. Perhaps she had heard him telling her, "I have called you by name; you are mine" (Isaiah 43:1, NLT). In any case, what Diane really wanted and needed was to embrace God's love, learn to treat herself with respect, and guard her inner sanctum for Christ alone. It would require letting go of what she could not control, holding on to her right to make choices, and discernment to tell the difference between the two.

The next time I saw Diane, I noted a change in her countenance. She appeared less desperate, more peaceful. Diane unfolded her story of the last few days, and I was struck by my own lack of faith as I anxiously awaited a report on whether she'd been seeing Jim. Instead, I was humbled by an honest account of what God can do, and often does, when we remove ourselves from the herd, draw away from the noisy clomping of hooves and whinnies that demand our attention, and hear the voice of the Holy Whisperer, who invites us to "join up" and again walk closely with him.

"I truly do care for Jim, Brenda," Diane said. "And I wanted more than anything to be with him. But when you said the word *affair*, it jarred me into thinking twice about what I was about to do. I was uncertain enough that I put Jim off that night and decided to pray for him instead."

"What?" I asked. My bottom jaw must have dropped a few inches.

Pausing, Diane reached inside her purse and withdrew a small book, *The Prayer of Jabez*. "Remember I told you Jim seemed to be God's answer to my prayers for a friend?"

"Yes, I remember."

"Well, I decided to pray for him until my confusion

passed and leave all my options open. Each morning last week I asked God to bless Jim, to bless him indeed, and to keep evil far from him that he might not have pain. In the process, something amazing happened. I realized that I might have become the personification of evil in his life. I might have been the reason for his downfall and destroyed two families for a moment's pleasure." Diane paused for a few seconds with eyes glistening and then added, "That's not really the kind of person I want to be."

Diane's real strength lay in her ability and willingness to look inside herself and check her raging demand to have her own way. This helped her recognize that her fantasies distorted reality and kept her from living with integrity. In deciding to let go of her illusions about Jim and take responsibility for her actions, Diane was wielding the shield of self-protection. The choice to pray, which could have been motivated only by the Holy Spirit, interrupted the swelling waves of desire and the demand for immediate fulfillment and calmed her yearning into ripples long enough for Diane to see beyond the shores of today. What she chose to cling to and let go of would affect many lives.

Is there something you need to let go of so that you can be more truly alive, more responsive to Christ? Could it be a life-draining habit? an inappropriate relationship? Is there anything you need to leave behind because it reveals that you are living as "Theirs," by surrendering that inner place inside you to someone other than Christ, or "Mine," by letting your own desires—not Christ's—control your choices? If so, what must you do to really be "His"?

SURRENDERING OUR VULNERABILITIES

• • •

HOW DO YOU BECOME STRONGER AND WISER?

IS THERE A MAGIC KEY, OR IS IT . . .

THE SAME WAY A PEARL GROWS, AS LAYER

UPON LAYER OF LIFE FORMS AROUND A

KERNEL OF TRUTH AND STRENGTH?

Bill Zimmerman[11]

One winter day a friend shared with me how disappointed she felt because our friendship seemed to be breaking down and I no longer treated her with the attentiveness and priority I'd once so eagerly demonstrated. I realized there was truth to her words and didn't like the sound of them. Both of us had been under heavy loads of stress: she with a tense family relationship and I with a loved one near death in the hospital. My friend wanted to meet to be reassured about our mutual loyalty to one another and to pray together about the differences cropping up between us. I wanted solitude, rest, and time to think and pray alone.

As she explained her feelings of rejection, I began to feel emotionally smothered and noticed my words becoming increasingly defensive as I tried to explain my constraints of personal energy and time. I, who could write and speak about God's love, could not practice it when my friend appeared to need me most, and I could only guess what ghosts from times past might be whispering in our ears, causing reactions we didn't understand. I wanted to give her more, to somehow fix things quickly, to say the right words to smooth things over. I didn't like my limitations. Yet I was also trying to maintain personal integrity and a right sense of priority. It wasn't clear to me how to be "His."

In need of objective counsel, I sought out a spiritual mentor who was familiar with my vulnerabilities and strengths. I explained the dilemma and how I'd tried to gain my friend's understanding. I felt that if I had disappointed my friend with my limitations, I at least wanted to make sure she understood my viewpoint, accepted my reasoning. But try as I might, I could not make my friend see my perspective.

"What is *your* sin in the misunderstanding?" the mentor asked, confronting me directly.

"But I never meant any harm," I defended. After some

discussion, prayer, and tears, I realized that I had stepped into a place in my friend's heart that God wanted for himself. My behavior had invited her to depend on me for more than I could give, to look to me for wisdom I did not possess. I had also depended on her for things God wanted me to trust him for. What was my sin in the misunderstanding? Pride, idolatry, and self-pity, for starters.

In a moment of solitude my eyes fell on Isaiah 43:1: "O Israel, the Lord who created you says: 'Do not be afraid, for I have ransomed you. I have called you by name; you are mine'" (NLT). Both my friend and I belonged to God, and each of us wanted to follow his path for our lives. "Come to me," our Master called. *Will you?* Come now, just as you are, in your pride and self-pity. Give them to me. "I have called you by name; you are mine."

As time passed, my tears of repentance transformed into a sorrowful and reluctant unclenching of hands. It was time to sweep my heart clean and trust that Christ's own light would guide both my friend and me down our paths and provide the encouragement and support we both needed, in his ways. The frequent togetherness we had so relished was now teaching us that respect for each other's priorities and simultaneous honor for our God-given uniqueness would separate us more than in the past, at least for a time. As we prayed for each other and ourselves, leaving our relationship in God's hands, it was control we were letting go of—not our affection for each other. Months would pass before we would both begin to see how he was strengthening each of us in our areas of greatest vulnerability and making each of us more "His."

God's love extends far beyond our vulnerabilities, our failures, our needs, and he wants us to give them to him, to let go and trust him. In Matthew chapter 26 we see that Christ himself went through the ultimate agony of surrendering control of his life as he prayed in Gethsemane, "My Father! If it is possible, let this cup of suffering be taken away from me. Yet I want your will, not mine" (v. 39, NLT). Left alone by friends who could not stay awake to pray or understand the gravity of the hour, Jesus again cried out, "My Father! If this cup cannot be taken away until I drink it, your will be done" (v. 42, NLT).

Christ must have also experienced that same inner human struggle we encounter when things get intense, when we want to clench our hands, to be understood by our critics, our friends, to have things be different. And yet in the pinnacle moment of surrendered strength, Jesus gave up control in order that God be God. Henri Nouwen writes, "It is the agony of a God who depends on us to decide how to live out the divine presence among us. It is the agony of the God who, in a very mysterious way, allows us to decide how God will be God."[12]

In our Christian lives we gradually mature into a graceful surrender to doing what is right as God continually asks us, *Will you?* Perhaps one of the compensations for growing older is that after having the truth hammered into our souls for so long, we begin to get the picture that we don't know the answers for others' lives or even for our own apart from God's daily guidance. At great cost to himself, he has given us charge over the choices we make. When the highest aim of our hearts is to please him above all others—even when we are weak, afraid, and vulnerable and when we fumble around trying to do the right thing and still disappoint those we love—he gives us grace to say yes to his sovereignty. Yes to letting go of having it our way. "Yes—thy will, not mine, be done."

• • •

LOVE THE LORD GOD WITH ALL YOUR

PASSION AND PRAYER AND INTELLIGENCE

AND ENERGY. . . . LOVE OTHERS AS WELL

AS YOU LOVE YOURSELF.

Mark 12:30-31, *THE MESSAGE*

RESISTING THE "OFF WITH HER HEAD" SYNDROME

Nurturing the Spirit by Reclaiming the Body

• • •

OH MY GOD, LET ME BE

WHOLLY YOURS.

Madame Jeanne Guyon[1]

$\mathcal{L}$ate one morning in May, Frank and I arrived in Eureka Springs for our semiannual escape to the Ozarks, where the hills are alive with the sound of jazz bands, the aroma of delectable food artfully prepared, and endless scenes of natural beauty. What we need most in a time away from home is a wake-up call for our souls—a time to play, get a massage, enjoy art, music, and great food. We let our brains rest and roam free in their naturally dominant right hemispheres for a long weekend. Ahhh! What renewing relief it is to reconnect with life—body, mind, and spirit.

We checked into our favorite bedroom-away-from-home at the Heartstone Inn late in the afternoon, then laced up our walking shoes and set out for our first trek down Benton Street. After a lap around Little Eureka Lake and dinner at Ermilios, we decided to take in the latest tourist attraction—a local magic show. We settled into the crushed velour seats just in time to see the magician's bang-up introduction, complete with popping fireworks and colored smoke. The magic show began with a disappearing card trick, progressed to the white-rabbit-in- a-hat, and then to the grand finale—a variation of the lady in a box getting her head cut off.

The magician helped the woman inside the box. Then he donned a knight's helmet, drew a long shiny sword and shouted, "Off with her head!" A drum roll sounded in the background as he inserted the sword into the box and pulled the two sections apart. The audience gasped as the magician opened the smallest segment, revealing the lady's head. (She faced the crowd and smiled). Then he unlatched and lowered the side board of the longer section, revealing the rest of her, from the shoulders down.

As the curtain lowered at the end of the show, the audience applauded and children asked, "How'd he do that?" The magician's illusion had successfully entertained us, waking up the cells in the problem-solving left sides of our brains and simultaneously stirring up the creative juices on the right side.

The following day as I relaxed on the back porch at the Heartstone, a lingering memory of the "Off with Her Head" trick floated back to mind for some leisurely reflection, intermingling with thoughts of ways women often struggle to remain integrated—to keep all the parts of themselves connected—head (mind) to body and spirit. Contemporary versions of what might be termed an "Off with Her Head" syndrome are likely to cause a sense of emotional disconnectedness with oneself. Late nineteenth-century writer and philosopher William James describes this fragmentation so well in the German word *Zerrissenheit*—"torn-to-pieces-hood."[2] The "tricks" that lure women into this state of disconnectedness can be as puzzling as a magician's illusion and far less entertaining.

Perhaps the axe that "cut off" a woman's head (mind) from her body was a sexual trauma. The memories in her head were just too painful to remember, so she disconnected from them and stored pent-up feelings of toxic shame in the cells of her body. Maybe a childhood fall down a long flight of stairs got encoded into her brain and twenty years later is still sending a rush of panicky feelings through her body each time she even thinks about riding an elevator to the top of a high-rise building. Perhaps her body just wouldn't do what she thought it was "supposed to" do—have babies, be healed of a disease, or measure up to today's ideal version of the female body—so she began to hate it and mistreat it.

Who among us has today's cultural ideal of the female body we see on the covers of magazines? (Mine has always been too flat on top, too flabby on the bottom, and too lanky all over. What's your version of physical imperfection?) Even those who manage to come close to the ideal find it's an ever-changing mirage: Marilyn Monroe's five-foot-four, one-hundred-thirty-five-pound body was later considered fat when the Twiggy look came into vogue. Later still the "ideal" shifted again to the Cindy Crawford look of today.

In our culture we're a lot like Alice in Lewis Carroll's *Through the Looking Glass*; we take great interest in things that shrink and grow us— often looking t the size of our bodies as the golden key to Wonderland. We're in dire need of a peek through a new looking glass.

In our culture we're a lot like Alice in Lewis Carroll's *Through the Looking Glass*; we take great interest in things that shrink and grow us—often looking to the size of our bodies as the golden key to Wonderland. Perhaps life becomes dull, as Alice's did, and a woman gets caught up in chasing hurried white rabbits who are always late for important dates and finds herself lost in a forest of signposts pointing every which way as the direction to fulfillment. We're in dire need of a peek through a new looking glass.

DIVINE REALITY TRANSCENDS HUMAN SHAME

• • •

DO YOU NOT KNOW THAT YOUR BODY

IS A TEMPLE OF THE HOLY SPIRIT,

WHO IS IN YOU, WHOM YOU HAVE RECEIVED

FROM GOD? YOU ARE NOT YOUR OWN;

YOU WERE BOUGHT AT A PRICE.

THEREFORE HONOR GOD WITH YOUR BODY.

1 Corinthians 6:19-20

Women's struggles to live abundant lives inside their imperfect bodies can be traced to Old Testament times. Hannah, wife of Elkanah, was deeply grieved and relentlessly ridiculed because she was barren. In those days a woman's status was dependent on her having a body that would bear babies to carry on the family line. Those who could not do this were thought defective and carried a great deal of shame. (Though having babies is still important today, culture's emphasis has shifted from the body's ability to reproduce to its ability to seduce.) Peninnah, Elkanah's other wife, provoked Hannah and antagonized her until she wept bitterly and would not eat. Deeply troubled, Hannah prayed to the Lord for a son. In opening Hannah's womb and giving her a son, Samuel, the Lord delivered Hannah from a position of disgrace to a position of honor and strength (see 1 Samuel 1).

Like Hannah, my friend and spiritual mentor Nell, who died some time ago, had a body that once caused her shame. Overtaken with a crippling disease, rheumatoid arthritis, Nell's body wouldn't do what she wanted it to do and prayed it would do—get well. Nell had tried herbal cures that had worked for some people, been anointed with oil at healing services, had elders lay their hands on her, yet each time she prayed with faith to be healed, the answer was always no. Nell told me stories of her younger years, how during her high school days she had been a beauty queen because of her attractive body and how her asset later became a liability when the disease struck.

Nell had smiled lovingly as she recalled sincere Christian friends who guaranteed her body would be healed if only she would have enough faith. "They meant well," she said, "and I still pray for healing to this day. But God has his ways, and we don't really understand much about them." Over time Nell had learned to nurture her spirit by staying connected to friends and family, by phone if not through personal visits, and to care for her aching body by getting daily massages from her husband, Dick. Nell relished these moments of life although they were mixed with constant physical pain. The embarrassment and shame her body caused her gradually transformed into a quiet acceptance of the crumbling earthen vessel that enabled her to walk (which for her was actually rolling along in a motorized cart) and talk with God throughout her days until at last her body drew its final breath.

But some women, both in ancient and contemporary times, were not so easily delivered from the shame their bodies brought upon them. Gnarled limbs and empty wombs brought one kind of curse. A barren soul called for a different cure. Tamar, the beautiful daughter of King David, was requested to make food for her half-brother Amnon, who was pretending to be ill:

> Then Amnon said to Tamar, "Bring the food here into my bedroom so I may eat from your hand." And Tamar took the bread she had prepared and brought it to her brother Amnon in his bedroom. But when she took it to him to eat, he grabbed her and said, "Come to bed with me, my sister."
>
> "Don't, my brother!" she said to him. "Don't force me. Such a thing should not be done in Israel! Don't do this wicked thing. What about me? Where could I get rid of my disgrace?" . . . But [Amnon] refused to listen to her, and since he was stronger than she, he raped her.
>
> Then Amnon hated her with intense hatred.

In fact, he hated her more than he had loved her. Amnon said to her, "Get up and get out!"

"No!" she said to him. "Sending me away would be a greater wrong than what you have already done to me."

But he refused to listen to her. He called his personal servant and said, "Get this woman out of here and bolt the door after her." (2 Samuel 13:10-17)

Dear, beautiful Tamar. She must have felt so used. She ripped her beautiful ornamented virgin robe, put ashes on her head, and wailed loudly.

"Be quiet now, my sister," her brother Absalom told her after learning what had happened. "Don't take this thing to heart" (v. 20).

What? Don't take this thing to heart? How could she not? If she had known she was to *become* Amnon's meal, she surely would not have gone into his bedroom. But she trusted him. The royal family kept its secrets, and life went on. But what about Tamar's pain and the shame she now carried in her body?

We are not told exactly what became of this Tamar, but 2 Samuel 13:20 says that she "lived in her brother Absalom's house, a desolate woman." It's not hard to understand why a woman like Tamar might learn to hate her body, the source of her shame. There has always been only one cure for human shame, whether self-inflicted or imposed by others. We see it portrayed poignantly in the story of the Pharisees who caught a woman in the act of adultery and then brought her to Jesus for judgment. But instead of judging her, Jesus did something shocking. He confronted her *accusers* with their own wickedness. Since none of them were sinless either, no one lifted a hand to stone her, the punishment the law required. Then Jesus turned to the woman.

"Has no one condemned you?" he asked.

"No one, sir," she said.

"Then neither do I condemn you," Jesus declared. "Go now and leave your life of sin" (John 8:10-11).

Do you see the difference? Jesus doesn't say, "Shame on you!" He doesn't say, "Don't take this thing to heart!" Hardly. On the contrary, Christ himself took the shame of the adulteress to his heart—his very own—and paid for it with his own body. The divine reality of the Incarnation always transcends human shame. Jesus wants us to bring our wounded spirits, weary minds, and violated bodies to him to be laced back together with his tender love and filled full of his Spirit. He wants us to leave our patchwork pasts behind.

Yet many victimized Tamars and women caught in adultery wash out to sea, unable to clean up the black spill on the shores of their souls. Sometimes they pack their heads full of biblical truths about the gentle compassion of God while their souls shrivel. They don't allow their bodies to experience the reality of any of the tenderness they read about. A woman's own heart may continue to hold her own body in contempt in spite of the fact that God knows all things and is greater than all things (see 1 John 3:20).

Richard Rohr, retreat master and author of *Simplicity, the Art of Living,* suggests that we acknowledge the limits of a problem-solving society without denying its positive gifts. "We have to move in the direction of a more body-related therapy and in the process give more weight to the right half of the brain."[3] This is not a new thought. Remember Christ's example of humility as he refreshed the disciples by washing their feet (see John 13:2-14)? Or Mary's coming to Jesus with an alabaster flask of costly perfume, pouring it on Jesus' head as he reclined at a table (see John 12:3)? These practices from olden times nurtured the spirit in physical ways through kindness and care to the body.

Serena is a contemporary Tamar—a woman once shamed because of what happened involuntarily to her body. Yet today she lives a fruitful spiritual life inside the same body that once cloaked her in shame, and with a mind that remembers why. It had been a painful passage for Serena to begin to feel again, to awaken to the longings of her heart after numbing them for decades following sexual trauma during her childhood. Once she did begin to experience feelings she'd shut away somewhere in the shadow of her soul all those years, she realized that she could not find complete fulfillment of her longing for intimacy with others and with God in this life. *Why did I bother to awaken to these feelings?* she questioned, bewildered. But God was shaking her awake to the realization that despite pain and tragedy, life is still worth experiencing, expressing, and celebrating.

As we sat together, Serena had poured out the grievous feelings in her heart, wept bitterly, angrily mocked the words from both Scripture and friends who wanted to encourage her because she couldn't reconcile those words of encouragement with what had happened to her body in the past. She had filled a spiral notebook with journaling to help her practice positive, truthful thinking habits and to separate today's realities from her past trauma. She'd also put together a scrapbook of photos, making a timeline to help place her past experiences in order.

Now Serena was reclaiming her body—the body she had rejected for years, the body she once refused to take care of because she felt it had betrayed her. She began to talk with me about the comfort she found for her artist's soul through painting, poetry, and dance, describing how she often choreographed movements that fit her mood. In Nikos Kazantzakis's novel *Zorba the Greek,* the title character expressed the gamut of his emotions through dance. If you remember the story, Zorba had to dance when he was "full," or else he felt as if he'd "burst." Even when his little son became sick and died, Zorba danced, expressing through his movements the pain of his broken heart.[4] In the same way, through dance Serena was finding a way to express her grief over her loss of childhood innocence and her joy in accepting God's tender loving-kindness. Although I was not accustomed to having clients dance in my office, Serena wanted to show me how she was experiencing a form of healing as she physically released her soul's lament through body movements.

She switched on the desktop tape recorder, smoothed her skirt with her hands, pushed her hair back from her face and smiled nervously, and then lifted her eyes as if a distant lover had drawn her gaze. As the music played,

Serena began to sway back and forth. Arms raised, hands gracefully outstretched heavenward, she stepped slowly, dramatically, across the room to the tune of Pachelbel's *Canon,* resembling a ballerina bride in waiting. With her hands over her heart, she slowly knelt, as if to pray, then stood and brushed her hands across her arms, touched her heart again, and with palms up she raised her hands as if to say, *Jesus, I belong to you—my heart, my mind, and my body.* Tears glistened in her eyes as her slender body U-turned into a low bow, hands to the floor, forehead to ankles, hair cascading to the floor as the canon ended.

Through dance, Serena's movements and facial expressions bypassed the need for words and explanations. They came from her deepest self, demonstrating her acceptance of truths she'd longed to really believe and know about God and his tender care for her. Frederick Buechner said, "All real art comes from the deepest self—painting, writing, music, dance. Our truest prayers come from there, too. And from there also come our best dreams and our times of gladdest play."[5] The biblical knowledge Serena had collected in her head over the fifteen years she had been a Christian was now released to flow into expressive movements through her torso, arms, fingers, legs, and toes. For Serena, a more "body-related therapy, giving more weight to the right half of the brain" as Richard Rohr suggested, was helping her reconnect with her deepest self and with God.

RECONNECTING BODY, MIND, AND SPIRIT

• • •

OUR SOUL IS BOWED DOWN TO THE DUST;

OUR BODY CLINGS TO THE GROUND.

ARISE FOR OUR HELP, AND REDEEM US

FOR YOUR MERCIES' SAKE.

Psalm 44:25-26, NKJV

Women's bodies pay a high price these days when they become disconnected from the rest of themselves. The immune system can be left vulnerable to attack following psychological distress, sometimes provoking conditions such as Chronic Fatigue Syndrome, Epstein-Barr virus, and fibromyalgia.[6] In *The Hidden Link between Adrenaline and Stress,* psychology professsor and author Dr. Archibald Hart describes the serious effects of persistently elevated levels of the stress hormone, especially on a person's heart and arteries.

The body's adrenaline response needs to be reserved for true emergencies, to calm the body and lower cholesterol and stress levels. Dr. Hart calls adrenaline "the Paul Revere of the body, heralding the approach of danger."[7] Recent research reveals that women who experienced shame, neglect, and abuse as children are conditioned to actually carry the effects of that ill treatment in the cells of their bodies as well as in their minds.[8] Our beliefs eventually move from being held only in our minds to taking on a physical aspect as our bodies try to cope with the stressors we have faced.

Our bodies have important things to say to us, and it is wise to listen to them: slowing down when they are fatigued, giving them what they need to be healthy, and letting them be the recipients of some of the tender care of Christ we often keep sequestered in our heads.

This may sound discouraging, as if you're under a death sentence if you didn't have a happy childhood. But as we make new choices and learn different behaviors, we can change our old ways of coping and interrupt the unhealthy cycles in which we have found ourselves in the past. Sometimes people need to incorporate forms of body-related therapy in their healing process. Others need help with redirecting their thoughts, actions, and behavior. Our bodies have important things to say to us, and it is wise to listen to them: slowing down when they are fatigued, giving them what they need to be healthy, letting them be the recipient of some of the tender care of Christ we often keep sequestered in our heads. Then our bodies can reserve the adrenaline response for its true purpose.

Eating Disorders

Eating disorders are further evidence of a disconnection between bodies, minds, and souls and of a lack of congruence between thoughts, feelings, and behavior. Many committed Christian women do not know how to integrate the information in their well-stocked minds into a more holistic, noncompartmentalized spiritual way of living that brings a sense of well-being to their bodies as well as to their minds and souls. They may know in their heads that their souls are eternally saved from hell and be able to cite the Bible verses to prove it. But when it comes to embracing God's mercy, their bodies are strangely off-limits.

Carmen was an attractive college student who had unconsciously "cut off," or disassociated, the truths she knew in her head from the body she had long detested. Although Carmen had an attentive and fun-loving boyfriend, a job that fit her natural strengths, and supportive Christian friends, her schedule and priorities revolved around twice-a-day, hour-and-a-half-long workouts. She had become driven by an endless blur of work, workouts, and power bars. When Carmen did take the time and effort to feed herself a healthy meal, she often overstuffed her body and then sent the food spewing back up in a rage she had disconnected from emotional pain and anxiety.

As a young child Carmen had been very fearful of her stepdad. One day she offhandedly told me about a girlhood habit she recalled: she would eat handfuls of strawberries just before her stepdad was coming to pick her up because they would make her break out in a rash and then her mom wouldn't make her go to her stepdad's house. A vague association between food, love, and her body began early in Carmen's life, and she learned that eating could gain her something or get her out of something with a person she both loved and hated. This was an important discovery for Carmen because it enabled her to identify an old, ineffective cycle of behavior that she needed to interrupt and change.

Carmen often mechanically recited Scripture verses to herself just before purging and then wondered why the Bible verses didn't empower her to stop making herself throw up. "First Corinthians 10:13 says, 'God is faithful, who will not allow you to be tempted beyond what you are able, but with the temptation will also make the way of escape, that you may be able to bear it.' But it's not working for me," she angrily lamented. Meanwhile she continued to overstuff and overwork her body relentlessly and cram her closet full of the latest fashions from her most recent shopping binge, intent on making a knockout impression at all costs.

Calling on "emergency" verses in moments of crisis had become Carmen's cloaked way of avoiding painful feelings and reality. But although God's living Word empowers his people, he will not be used or manipulated. As a result, the knowledge in Carmen's head had become stagnant, like the Dead Sea—full of accumulated minerals but empty of anything alive. Carmen needed to find ways to stay emotionally connected to herself, to God, and to other people and to integrate her honest feelings, thoughts, and behavior into a healthier and more biblical lifestyle.

Carmen and I discussed ways to break her old, ineffective cycle of behavior and redirect herself in healthier ways—calling a friend, journaling about her feelings, or taking a walk when she experienced anxiety instead of anesthetizing it. We prayerfully called on God for his intervention, wisdom, and guidance. Each time Carmen was able to choose a new response by redirecting her behavior, she experienced a victory, even if for only a few minutes. She switched from her hard-driving workouts to a Jazzercise class three or four times a week. Incorporating dance into her exercise routine added a shot of fun to her days and also did something good for her body. As time passed, Carmen began to relate to friends and family differently, with more integrity. And as she became more aware of God's presence and care for her, she connected with him emotionally as well as intellectually, and her prayers more often included expressions of gratitude.

Nurturing Your Spirit

Like many other women, you may need to search for ways to put the truths you know in your head into practice so that they make a real difference in your overall way of living. As we work on nurturing our spirits, God "regathers" the various facets of who we are as individuals, the way he did the nation of Israel in the Bible. There we see that when the people of Israel were scattered, wandered off, or were exiled from their homeland, it was always the longing of God's loving heart—and his promise—to bring them back together so that he could bless them. In a similar way, as we nuture our spirits, we become more integrated physically, mentally, and spiritually, and we are able to rest more completely in God.

Ultimately, God in his sovereignty may work through even a debilitating illness such as Chronic Fatigue Syndrome or fibromyalgia to draw his dear children closer to his heart. Some women who have studied their energy-depleting illnesses and done all they could to take care of themselves and become more integrated still remain unhealed. And yet they describe their suffering as "the thing that holds me close to God." We can only marvel, wonder, and bow to such divine mysterious workings when we see them. And from these workings we can learn that there are no limits to what God will do in his loving pursuit of us.

Can you name two or three things that nurture your spirit? Are you spending time doing these things? Perhaps you are not a trauma victim or an artist or a dancer, but you can learn to listen to your body and let it tell you what it needs. You can also make intentional efforts to care for your body through relaxing, appropriate touch, lotions and bubble baths, whatever expresses respect and honor for your body. If you were to really listen to what your body was saying to you, what would you do differently? What would you do more of? less of? The body is often our best source of information about how much of anything—food, exercise, shopping, service to others—is "enough."

We all need to be aware of physical activities that feel comfortable and good to us. As you do them, ask yourself, *What am I feeling? How do I want to respond, express, or relish this experience?* As you feed your body healthy food, try eating more slowly, noticing the texture of the food, savoring the smells as well as the tastes. When you exercise, let your body tell you when to slow down the pace and when it has had "enough."

Torn-to-Pieces-Hood

In what ways do you think you might suffer from the disease of disconnection? I don't think anyone in our culture totally escapes it. For me, an ineffective cycle that would eventually lead to torn-to-pieces-hood began in junior high, during a time when I felt isolated and disconnected from my family. Before long I had lost my sense of connection to myself.

One day a strange silence fell over our home. My parents and older sister, Jan, held secret meetings behind closed doors. Often my mother came out of the room crying, and my dad looked very sad. I could tell something was terribly wrong, but nobody talked about it. A few days later my dad told me that Jan was getting married, and I felt happy until I realized it would mean she was moving away. Then I was sad too.

Mother and Dad were brokenhearted after Jan left, and I wondered what I could do to make them happy again. I decided to do what my sister would have done—try to be popular and become a cheerleader. I put my dance leotard and flute away in the closet, started studying harder so I could make better grades, and smiled at everyone I met in the school hallways. It took a couple of years, but my plan worked, and my parents were proud and happy again. My sister had a baby now, and they both moved back in with us after she was divorced. My nephew was really more like a little brother, and sometimes they all came to watch me lead cheers at the football games. Now I was very much loved for being what I was not.

As years passed, I became firmly established in an ineffective cycle of responding obediently but mechanically to
those who said they loved me, even God, while feeling
emotionally disconnected from them as well as from
myself. This wasn't something I did intentionally. It was a
subtle, illusory trick. While I went through the motions of
a lot of right behaviors—rigidly following rules, filling my
mind with good and truthful thoughts—I lost track of my
true self. As Dallas Willard writes in *The Divine Conspiracy,*
"The keeping of the law turns out to be an inherently
self-refuting aim; rather, the inner self must be changed.
Trying merely to keep the law is not wholly unlike trying to
make an apple tree bear peaches by tying peaches onto its
branches."[9]

Try as I might to be a peach tree, I was an apple
bearer. Once I accepted God's acceptance of me as an
imperfect human being who often makes mistakes, the
newfound intimacy of my grace-based connection with
him helped me also accept others in "as is" condition.
My sister was very, very Jan, and I was very, very Brenda,
and each of us had been given the job of being distinctly
ourselves.

Christ changed my inner self gradually as I became
convinced that he accepted me completely, regardless of
how empty or full my head was, how fit or fat my body was,
and how right or wrong my behavior was. Ironically, once
I sensed his deep love for me, I wanted to be my best for
him. But this time I wanted it from my heart; it was no
longer merely a mechanical response. With that new
motivation I began to relate to my sister and to others in a
new and deeper way, without competition and comparison.

As I related to Jan in a more genuine way, she and I
moved toward mutual acceptance, and that helped me feel
more connected not only to her but also to all of humanity
as I felt more compassionate about the joys and sorrows of
others. The pressure I had once felt to keep all the rules
and hold to a rigid routine in my spiritual life began to feel
binding, like too-tight elastic belting my soul, and I was

finally released to practice more creative forms of discipline. The neat, tidy, preppy way I'd always dressed evolved into a preference for more flowing gauzy skirts and blouses. The physical, emotional, and spiritual aspects of my life became more integrated and flexible as I experienced increased connectedness with God, with my true self, with other people, and with my surroundings. I even resumed playing the flute in my early forties as a fun way of expressing creativity, joy, and worship.

Frank and I recently moved to the historic district of McKinney, Texas. We love the eclectic neighborhood, tree-lined streets, clotheslines, and picket fences. I often take brisk morning walks with my dog, Molly. We head down Tucker Street and make a three-mile loop, altering our route to check out new streets if beckoned by colorful flowers or an intriguing old house we haven't seen. Smelling the flowers, greeting people out changing the water in their birdbaths or setting sprinklers, and enjoying the birds are more important than making sure I've walked exactly three miles in forty minutes.

The stresses of life on our bodies will always be present, whether we live in the heart of a big city or nestled in the midst of the Ozarks. But one day our souls will take leave of these tattered bodies, fly away, and be transformed for all eternity. Won't it be wonderful? Percy Bysshe Shelley wrote these words about "unbodied joy" in his poem *To a Skylark:*

> In the golden lightning
> Of the sunken sun,
> O'er which clouds are brightening,
> Thou dost float and run,
> Like an unbodied joy whose race is just begun.[10]

We can only imagine what joy will be ours when these days of the Meantime are over and God clothes us in our new, heavenly bodies. Until that day, let us welcome his care for our whole selves, keep learning the truth, teach our minds to share with our bodies and spirits. Let us honor and

respect our imperfect clay jars, including them in the joyful experience of belonging to Christ here and now.

• • •

WE HAVE THIS TREASURE IN JARS

OF CLAY TO SHOW THAT THIS

ALL-SURPASSING POWER IS FROM GOD

AND NOT FROM US.

2 Corinthians 4:7

AWAKENING TO THE KING'S KISS

Reigniting Passion for God

• • •

It was two weeks before Valentine's Day, my youngest son's senior year in high school. I had just mailed a batch of handmade invitations to a candlelight dinner Frank and I were planning for a few couples, and I'd clipped a recipe for a do-ahead chicken cordon bleu casserole from *Southern Living*. As I grabbed my purse from the kitchen countertop and dug around for the car keys, grocery list in hand, a few last-minute necessities came to mind, so I added them to the bottom of the list: heart-shaped doilies, red netting, ribbon to tie up table favors of sweetheart candies.

This was to be a romantic gathering honoring passionate love—love between husbands and wives and ultimately between our Lord and us—his children. Sally was to bring red place cards with 1 Corinthians 13 scrolled in heart-shaped designs to set atop the white linen tablecloths. Jill, a kindred romantic, would bring some little books of love poems to set around. I'd rummaged through each room in our house and collected a small mound of heart-shaped picture frames, candleholders, and old valentines. Anticipation mounted as our plans for the special occasion unfolded. Frank would strum his guitar and sing "My Sweet Lady," and I would recite a poem I'd recently written. In the company of good friends it would be a perfect evening.

SPIRITUAL INFATUATION

The poem I had written—in King James language to make sure God knew I meant business—was a cry for him to rekindle my passion, to wake me up, to somehow revive me with a few puffs of holy CPR as I felt my heart growing icy cold and slipping into what Brennan Manning calls a "faith crisis" in his book *The Ragamuffin Gospel.* He uses those words to describe "the point at which it would no longer be okay to go on giving lip service to what was not really true for me."[2] I had come to that point after realizing that I'd spent the early years of my Christian life in spiritual infatuation—in love with the idea of loving God. I had begun immersing myself in the writings of Amy Carmichael and Madame Jeanne Guyon and felt unfamiliar with the kind of passion they expressed. These women were on fire for God, as the psalmist was when he penned, "As the deer pants for streams of water, so my soul pants for you, O God" (Psalm 42:1).

Just as Sleeping Beauty's slumber could be broken only by a kiss from the king's son, so our souls can be awakened only by the Son of God.

Over the next two years I would begin to discover the difference between spiritual infatuation with God based on my ability to love him well, and the kind of enduring romance that flows from the passionate heart of a God who cannot hold himself back from loving the unlovely. Just as Sleeping Beauty's slumber could be broken only by a kiss from the king's son, so our souls can be awakened only by the Son of God.

Up until the time my children left home and I entered my "faith crisis," I had only scratched the surface of understanding that "Father knows best." I had no clue that passion was often borne more of sorrow than of idealized romanticism; more akin to slaves singing "Nobody Knows de Trouble I've Seen" than the syrupy scenes that Jane Wyman and Robert Young played out on the television set during my growing-up years. In asking God to rekindle my passion for him, I had unknowingly begged him to awaken me to my desperate need of him. Christ is the embodiment of passion, and it is only in getting a true picture of *his* passion, *his* suffering, that we become passionate people.

During the first six or seven years Frank and I were married, God had blessed us abundantly in ways we could comprehend. The two of us shared common interests, our kids were doing well, our work was rewarding and promised a stable financial future, and we were in good health. We were so grateful for our life of blessing. I still recall one particular evening when we decided to pray a prayer of "total commitment," asking God to make us totally his, no matter what it took.

Almost immediately the tide of our lives began to turn. Frank's work in the restoration of classic cars suddenly took a nosedive. I left my position after seven years as secretary to the headmaster at a Christian school to allow my youngest son, Brent, a little more independence during his final two years of high school because he seemed to need the space. I prayed for God's guidance, but the two jobs I tried next turned out to be disasters.

I had heard the scriptural account of Christ's dying on the cross for my sins many times since the day when I first responded to it by asking Christ to be my Savior. But as disappointments, letdowns, and failures stacked up alongside blessings in forms I could recognize, my heart response to Christ had grown dull, limp, lifeless. We kept praying for guidance, reaching out for God, asking friends to pray for us. Yet the further we reached, the further away God seemed to move, always just beyond our grasp, out of the range of our sight and earshot. It was at this time that I'd written the poem asking God to reignite my spiritual passion, hoping to get his attention.

I had been trying my hardest to love God, to serve him well, to have strong faith, but nothing worked. God appeared to be taking everything away from me until finally I became so disillusioned that if it were possible to throw in the spiritual towel, I'd have done it. Then one day, at the very moment of my greatest frustration and disillusionment, I let loose at God in a way I'd never had the nerve to do before—*Hello? God? Are you even there? You say you love me. You call this love?* At that very moment—when it finally became crystal clear to me that I had no virtue of my own, that without God all I could ever expect to be was depressed, isolated, and confused—in that very moment the passion of Christ broke through my heart's crust of concealed pride and convinced me of the depth of my need for his grace.

Suddenly I knew that this was the same passion Christ had, the passion that sent him to the cross, kept him hanging there in agony, crying out to his Father, by whom he felt forsaken. That same passion was now coming to me personally, convincing me of his love because I needed him so much that I wasn't going to make it without him.

Until that time, I hadn't especially thought I really needed God's grace. I didn't realize this, couldn't have explained it, and you wouldn't have seen it from the outside. But it was a hidden heart condition waiting to be exposed to me so that I could believe—really believe—that Jesus loves me. Seeing Christ's passion, not only for all humankind but also for me personally, ignited a flame of passion in my own heart and created a longing to serve him, to know him, to give myself to him in a way I'd not understood before.

We need to realize, however, that looking for fulfillment by attaining a state of passionate love for God is not the same as seeking God for *his* sake—loving, serving, and worshiping him because he is God. I doubt that in all the days of Jesus' life here on earth he had even a moment's concern about whether his own passion for God was being kindled. It just happened as he lived for his Father, looked to him, and trusted him. As we see how Christ fleshed out God's love for humankind, we begin to move past our egocentric notions about fulfillment and passion, our shallow understandings of where it all starts and ends. When spiritual infatuation burns out, what's left is love—agape love—self-giving love. In the same way that a mother's milk nourishes her baby, the realization of God's unmerited love for us enlivens our souls in a way nothing else can. The kiss of grace is something we can never predict or deserve or earn. We can only recognize our desperate need of God and put ourselves in a place where he can get at us, and when we do, we begin to grow in grace.

GROWING IN GRACE

• • •

HOW OFT I WAKE AND FIND I HAVE
BEEN FORGETTING THEE. I AM NEVER FAR
FROM THY MIND; THOU IT IS THAT WAKEST ME.

George Macdonald[3]

To be needy, something those who want to be "spiritually strong" may not find attractive, is not only fine with God, it is the prerequisite to really seeing Jesus as the only One who can day by day reignite spiritual passion within our hearts. In *We Would See Jesus,* authors Roy and Revel Hession write: "Where there is need, there is God. Where there is sorrow, misery, unhappiness, suffering, confusion, folly, oppression, there is the I AM, yearning to turn man's sorrow into bliss whenever man will let Him. It is not, therefore, the hungry seeking for bread, but the Bread seeking the hungry; not the sad seeking for joy, but rather Joy seeking the sad; not emptiness seeking fullness, but rather Fullness seeking emptiness. And it is not merely that He supplies our need, but He becomes Himself the fulfillment of our need."[4]

If we do not recognize our desperate need of God, we don't recognize him as the fulfillment of our desperate

To be needy, something those who want to be "spiritually strong" may not find attractive, is not only fine with God, it is the prerequisite to really seeing Jesus as the only One who can day by day reignite spiritual passion within our hearts.

need, and that blocks us from receiving that fulfillment. Our eyes remain blind to his grace, our ears do not hear his voice, our minds are dulled, our spirits are closed when he passes by. God is still there, but we are just not awake to his presence.

When we came into the world as babies, our spirits were open. But over the years we collected some hurts, disappointments, rejections, and our spirits began to close up. Well-known author and speaker Gary Smalley teaches married couples how to help reopen their spouses' closed spirits by being attentive and receptive to each other, by show-ing interest and affection. He uses the illustration of an open hand to symbolize an open spirit; a clenched fist to represent a closed spirit. The simple illustration is intended to help couples grow more aware of whether they are inviting openness and receptiveness or causing their spouses to with-draw and close up.

In our relationship with God we can come to him as dependent little children, asking him to open our spirits so we can grow in his grace, to give us eyes to see and ears to hear him through life's ups and downs. As wounds come, we can bring our closed spirits back to him for healing and reopening so that we can again become vulnerable to those around us as we continually entrust ourselves to the safe-keeping of God's presence. Though it's not consistently true of people, the Holy Spirit is always open, always ready to give us love, always dependably there, whether it feels like it to us or not. I didn't really know this or understand how to live in the light of this truth until Christ's passion was revealed to me. That day on my deck (described in chapter 2), I had unknowingly placed myself where God could "get at" me.

How are you opening yourself to God so that he can get at you in this way in your life? When we pray, we make ourselves available to God, reopen our spirits to him, tell him, "Here I am, Lord." We may need to talk something over with him, express praise, adoration, disappointment, grief. When we sit in silence, consciously opening ourselves to God's presence and to what he wants to reveal to us, we may find that he comes to us in a way that refreshes us spiritually and emotionally. Or perhaps he teaches us a new insight in prayer, as Isaiah said: "Morning by morning he wakens me and opens my understanding to his will" (Isaiah 50:4, NLT). But most of the time, we probably won't *feel* anything at all.

Often our communion with God's Spirit may even feel more like abandonment than rapture. But God wants us to simply, expectantly seek him because he is our God, not because of any certain kinds of feelings, rewards, or anything else we may get from it. As fourteenth-century English mystic Julian of Norwich writes, "God wishes to be seen, and he wishes to be sought, and he wishes to be expected."[5] As we keep seeking Christ, mindful of our need of him, and ask him to make us spiritually receptive, we can expect him to open our eyes and ears to new wonders of his grace.

EXPECTING GOD

• • •

THIRSTY HEARTS ARE THOSE WHOSE
LONGINGS HAVE BEEN WAKENED
BY THE TOUCH OF GOD WITHIN THEM.

A. W. Tozer[6]

Have you ever wondered how Mary must have felt when the angel appeared to her—a virgin—and announced that she would become pregnant with the Son of God? She was just an ordinary woman, quite young, preparing for marriage:

> "Greetings, you who are highly favored! The Lord is with you."
>
> Mary was greatly troubled at his words and wondered what kind of greeting this might be. But the angel said to her, "Do not be afraid, Mary, you have found favor with God. You will be with child and give birth to a son, and you are to give him the name Jesus. He will be great and will be called the Son of the Most High. The Lord God will give him the throne of his father David, and he will reign over the house of Jacob forever; his kingdom will never end."
>
> "How will this be," Mary asked the angel, "since I am a virgin?"
>
> The angel answered, "The Holy Spirit will come upon you, and the power of the Most High will overshadow you. So the holy one to be born will be called the Son of God. . . . Nothing is impossible with God."
>
> "I am the Lord's servant," Mary answered. "May it be to me as you have said." (Luke 1:28-38)

We're not surprised that Mary was "greatly troubled and wondered what kind of greeting this might be." Who wouldn't? And yet Mary responded to the angel's announcement with no apparent thought of how she would explain her virgin pregnancy to Joseph, her soon-to-be husband. That must have been an interesting conversation between Mary and Joseph, don't you think?

But then, the birth. The Christ child. Mary must have kissed the face of baby Jesus and sung to him and rocked him back and forth in her arms. She must have watched him growing up, getting taller and taller. Then, the day she and Joseph couldn't find Jesus, and they searched for him, finally finding him in the temple talking with the religious leaders. I wonder if Mary recalled the angel's words: *The Son of the Most High . . . His kingdom will never end.*

This was the Father's call that ultimately drew Jesus to agony on the cross.

Do you suppose Mary let out a heartrending scream as the son she'd given birth to hung on the cross dying? What mother wouldn't? She might even have rocked herself as she had rocked the child, and wailed and whimpered as she swayed back and forth in her grief. Mary—virgin mother of the Christ child, mourning mother of the slain Savior. What had it been like for her to be expectant with the Christ child and then to bear the birth and death of Passion Personified? How eagerly her unknowing response to the angel had sprung up from within: "I am the Lord's servant. May it be to me as you have said."

As Mary was impregnated by the Holy Spirit, so in each of us whose hearts are open to Jesus, Christ's love reaches deep down inside us seeking a dwelling place and fills us with expectant hope. And like Mary, we responsively give our hearts over to God's purposes in awe and wonder at being blessed women. We hear and see what God has for us when we come to him expectantly, or we miss what he has for us because we aren't waiting openly and expectantly. But each time the Holy Spirit awakens us to an awareness of his presence, our passion for God is rekindled.

GOD'S GRACE OPENS US TO NEW PERSPECTIVES

Barbara had suffered long bouts of depression throughout her life. Old conflicts between her and her mother remained unresolved, and as Barbara's preschool daughter grew old enough to sense the tension between Mommy and Grandma, Barbara realized something needed to change.

"Why can't my mom stop drinking?" Barbara lamented. "I know I can't change her, but I just don't understand how she can be so selfish!" Barbara's preschool-age daughter wanted to spend time alone with Grandma, to go shopping or have a special lunch together. But the last time Barbara had entrusted young Julie to Grandma's care, she had returned to find her mom drunk and little Julie with a stomachache from eating half a bag of

Tootsie Rolls. From that time on, the only way Barbara could ensure her daughter's safety was to supervise Julie's visits with Grandma.

With a previous counselor Barbara had mapped out a genogram showing her family's pattern of addiction. She was determined to break the cycle in her generation, yet her repressed anger hovered just below the boiling point most of the time. One day as I sat with Barbara, it occurred to me that learning about Barbara's family's addictive patterns had taken her a good way down the road to self-under-standing, but it really hadn't empowered her to move on to a better quality of life herself. "Would you consider trying to look at your family history in a new way?" I asked.

Clearly Barbara could do nothing to change her mom's drinking problem; she could only try to protect her daughter from it. But the real miracle was that God had opened and invaded Barbara's heart. Among all her family members, only two had come to know Christ, and when someone sees divine truth, it is always a miracle. "Who are the people who have been the 'historical markers' in your spiritual life?" I asked, thinking it might be helpful to "reframe" Barbara's perspective.

"In my spiritual life?" she asked. At first Barbara was puzzled, but after we discussed it briefly, she agreed to think about that question. During the next week Barbara thought of five women, including one relative on her dad's side of the family, who had had a significant impact on her faith in Christ. Aunt Sally had set a model of loving-kind-ness, sobriety, and active Christian faith. A work supervi-sor had taken Barbara to her first AA meeting, where she first gained support and strength to break her own alcohol addiction. A college professor had convinced her that she could pass physics. A friend had revived a love for music by teaching her to play the violin. And another had been a faithful prayer partner. As Barbara charted her own spiri-tual history, God opened her eyes to ways he had graciously intervened in her life, calling her out of the long estab-lished family-addiction patterns.

Barbara's new perspective didn't magically take away

her depression. It didn't create safety for Julie to be alone with her grandma. But it did renew a little verve to Barbara's life as God's grace awakened her to a form of blessing she hadn't been aware of before. As she developed the expectation of seeing the good things God had done for her, she was more alert to his presence and his loving interventions in her life, and her attitude began to make the shift from one of resentment to one of gratitude.

Just as it was helpful to Barbara to look at things from a different perspective, sometimes we need to begin to see things from a different perspective as well, always truth-based, of course, just from a wider angle of awareness of God's grace. Is there some way you might benefit or grow closer to God if you looked at things from a different point of view? Perhaps you have become so focused on what you *don't* have that you can't see what's right in front of you. Even if you have a past strewn with painful relationships, try naming some ways God has used less-than-ideal people and circumstances to make you more like Christ. Once you see these manifestations of God's grace, your hurts, fears, and resentments will begin to transform into gratitude to God for his workings in your life, just as they did for Barbara.

PASSION THROUGH THE AGES

• • •

GOD IS NOT SEEN EXCEPT BY BLINDNESS,

NOR KNOWN EXCEPT BY IGNORANCE,

NOR UNDERSTOOD EXCEPT BY FOOLS.

Meister Eckhart[7]

Each day brings new mercies, good-morning "kisses" from our Father that awaken us to see the spontaneous joy of a child or the mysterious contentment of an elderly woman in a great deal of pain who is patiently waiting to die. Perhaps a heart that has grown passionate for God is most evident in old people. Inside a sharp but slowed-down mind and a timeworn body, little else is left except the life force that shines out through the windows of the soul, reflecting the openness or closed state of the spirit. If the fires of passion have not been rekindled occasionally over the years, it's hard to hide it when you're old.

"How are you feeling today, Aunt Joella?" I asked as I entered the rehab quarters where my eighty-eight-year-old nearly-blind aunt was recovering from a recent fall.

"Oh, I'm doing really good today," she replied. "I'll be out of here in no time."

"Are you having trouble keeping your hands warm again?" I asked, noting the gloves she'd been told to wear to improve circulation in her fingers.

"Yes, the gloves work better than a sink full of hot water." After a report on the day's menu and visitors, Aunt Joella told me how her fingers had begun to turn blue that afternoon and she'd rung the buzzer but the nurses were all busy. "So, I started thinking, *Now what would Mother do to take care of me if she were here?* I knew she would tell me to put my hands in some warm water, so that's what I did." The fruits of many years of childlike trusting and obeying were now fully ripened, golden apples of grace falling down around my aunt to refresh others.

"Did you get any sleep last night?" I asked.

"Oh, you know old people hardly ever sleep," she said with a slight smile.

"What do you do all night, just lie here and think?"

"Yes, it's not really so bad."

"What do you think about?"

"Well, I think about the good life the Lord has given me," my aunt replied. "I think about the little dandelions Jimmy used to bring to me and the love notes Sonny used to write me and the pictures I've saved from when they were little boys." Aunt Joella seemed to have always known she needed God. Yet even with him, hers was to be a life of intermingled joy and sorrow; she had buried both of her sons during the previous two years.

Frank had come with me to visit her the day before. "You'd better be practicing your singing, Frank," she had instructed. "I want you to sing 'Amazing Grace' at my funeral." After she'd hummed a couple of tunes to make sure Frank knew which were her favorites, we said good night.

Aunt Joella had walked long years with Someone passionate, and now it showed. Though her eyes were now blind, her spiritual vision was twenty-twenty. During recent years, Aunt Joella had done a lot of waiting: waiting to see doctors, waiting for the nurse to come and give her a bath, waiting to join her husband and sons in heaven—just waiting. But while she was waiting she was also available, awake, and ready for whatever was to come next. Expecting to find beauty in each day here—along with the inevitable pain—she taught us all to wait well, to live expectantly, to grow in grace, to look at the world through the eyes of a child.

Then one day Aunt Joella's soul slipped away into the Happily Ever After. Like a phantom Beauty sleeping still on the hospital bed, she had finally been visited by the King's Son and kissed awake into another life. Only a skeletal remembrance of her passion, once so alive, remained. Just as she had instructed, Frank sang about the sweet sound of the "Amazing Grace" of God at her funeral, choking up when he came to "was blind, but now I see." A teenage girl named Jessica gave a poignant tribute to Aunt Joella, known to her and half her hometown as "Maw-Maw." Jessica told of times she'd spent in Aunt Joella's apartment coloring and playing dolls and then in more recent years sharing secrets her single mom was too busy to hear. "Maw-Maw" had left a historical marker in young Jessica's life, and she wanted everybody to know it.

The stories that follow a person like Aunt Joella after they're gone remind us that a God of passion is present in the world, walking among us here and now. Sometimes God awakens us during a quiet moment as we sit still, pray, or listen to music. Other times he breaks through our resistance, overshadows us with his presence, or shows us a new perspective. As he grows us, he even gives us a more gracious spirit toward ourselves so that we can accept our lives as his workmanship. With gratitude we can stand in awe of a God who doesn't grade our prayers or take points off because we had our focus a bit off center. He delights in our prayers, and it is always right to pray. Each time we give our hearts to him, he is well pleased. To him, awakening us spiritually is not about our becoming more advanced in our prayer life or deeper or better at it. It's about belonging to him and about *his* passionate desire to respond to our desperate need.

As I look back on that poem I wrote to share at our Valentine party some years ago, in which I asked God to rekindle my spiritual passion, I can't say I know God did it in answer to my prayer—perhaps he had it all planned anyway. Frederick Buechner writes in *The Magnificant Defeat*, "Not knowing is what makes today a holy mystery as every day is a holy mystery."[8] I can only smile as I see it from both perspectives—then and now—and trust that there was a time for each way of looking at it.

Whether the emphasis is on my ability to love him well or on his pursuit of my heart, he understands. He wants only for us to give him our hearts. He takes them and makes something good out of our little offerings and blesses us in ways we never could have imagined. That's what we can expect from our King.

Kindle my passion for Thee, my King,
Let Thy strength be found in me;
All glory be Thine, and if Thou desire,
My weakness be plain to see.

Kindle my passion for Thy living word
Apart from which is naught;
Send me Thy wisdom to be my guide
And by it my spirit be taught.

My thoughts wander far from Thee, my King,
And forget Thy good, kind ways.
Call to me often and cause me to see
Thy faithfulness in all of my days.

Kindle my passion for Thee, my King,
Bring me no praise of men.
Let pride not take what belongs to Thee
Nor destroy what Thou wouldst win.

• • •

WE THINK PRAYER IS OUR REACHING

OUT TO GOD. BUT IT TURNS OUT TO BE

GOD'S SPIRIT MOVING IN US.

Ann and Barry Ulanov[9]

ENTERING THE CASTLE OF PEACE

Finding the Safe Retreat of Stillness and Solitude

• • •

"THE GOSPEL" IS THE GOOD NEWS OF THE
PRESENCE AND AVAILABILITY OF LIFE
IN THE KINGDOM, NOW AND FOREVER,
THROUGH RELIANCE ON JESUS THE ANOINTED.

Dallas Willard[1]

Recently one evening as we sat down to relax after dinner, my oldest son, Scott, announced the happy news that he and his girlfriend, Jane, were planning a wedding to be held in about three months. They wanted to keep it simple, for family only, and they would invite friends to join them for a party following the ceremony. Jane and I shrieked with glee, we all hugged, and visions of grandchildren danced in my head.

A few days later Jane and I started discussing plans for the wedding, her dress, invitations, the cake, flowers, all the details that we would have to work out, even for a simple celebration. Jane's mom (mum) lives in England, so Nancy (Scott's stepmom) and I were to share the joyful role of mother of the bride. Soon our lists of things to do grew lengthy, more people became involved in the planning, and we all felt the stress as we tried to balance planning the ceremony with our jobs, household responsibilities, and the needs of friends and family.

One morning when my alarm went off quite early, I dragged myself out of bed, turned on the coffeepot, slumped into my prayer chair, and clicked on the lamp. The tension in my shoulders and the mental clatter of reminders of must-dos accentuated the contrast between my state of being and the "quiet time" I was attempting to enter into. Even when I was sitting still, taking slow deep breaths, trying to open my heart to God, the noisy thoughts in my head would not stop spinning.

Ironically, in addition to my role in helping with wedding plans, the deadline for the book you are holding in your hands loomed just weeks away, and in one month I was to lead my first retreat on reflective living. "Jesus, calm my anxious heart," I whispered numbly. What did I know about the reflective life at a time like this, when I felt so tossed about by the details and busyness of my days?

Suddenly I thought of the fearful disciples in the boat with Jesus when he stilled the wind and the seas, and I looked up the passage in Mark 4: "A great windstorm arose, and the waves beat into the boat, so that it was already filling. But He was in the stern, asleep on a pillow. And they awoke Him and said to Him, 'Teacher, do You not care that we are perishing?'" Oh yes, I could relate to these words. They came alive as I read on: "Then He arose and rebuked the wind, and said to the sea, 'Peace, be still!' And the wind ceased and there was a great calm" (vv. 37-39, NKVJ).

A glimmer of hope arose in my heart that Jesus might calm my anxieties as he had stilled the waters around the disciples. Perhaps he was asleep and I just needed to wake him up and remind him how full my boat was getting. I kept reading: "He asked them, 'Why are you so afraid? Do you still not have faith in me?' And they were filled with awe and said among themselves, 'Who is this man, that even the wind and waves obey him?'" (vv. 40-41, NLT). I hung on the words, wondering why the story had stopped there, with so many things left unsaid, so many questions left unanswered.

I looked up the passage in a couple of other translations hoping to gain some insight into faith in the midst of stormy and busy times. The same passage in *The Message* says this: "Awake now, [Jesus] told the wind to pipe down and said to the sea, 'Quiet! Settle down!' The wind ran out of breath; the sea became smooth as glass. Jesus reprimanded the disciples: 'Why are you such cowards? Don't you have any faith at all?' They were in absolute awe, staggered. 'Who is this, anyway?'"

Then I began to notice some truths I had never seen before. After Jesus rebuked the disciples for their lack of faith, they didn't just settle down and get calm—it was the sea that became glassy smooth, not the disciples' nerves. They "were in absolute awe, staggered." Their fear did not merely die down; it transformed into holy awe. In that moment all my fears and hurry-ups and don't-forgets were suddenly stilled, smoothed, as I glimpsed the faithful Jesus at the stern of the boat. Whether he was awake or asleep, it was his *presence* that safeguarded the disciples' lives. Being with him was the only necessary thing.

Peace, be still. This time as I read those words, they met my soul in a different place as my focus shifted from what I wanted *from God* to the consolation of just *being with him*. In his presence I regained confidence that everything important to him would be accomplished in that day. My shoulders relaxed. My heart rate slowed. My thoughts returned to the joy of the wedding plans and the privilege of gaining a new daughter-in-law. I smiled as I envisioned the dinner party coming up and the dainty earrings I had wrapped the night before to give Jane as a special gift at the party. And anticipation and joy were renewed in the calming, restoring presence of Christ.

• • •

AS SOON, HOWEVER, AS WE SET OUR

HEARTS ON THESE THINGS [GOD'S KINGDOM]

OUR MINDS STOP SPINNING BECAUSE WE ENTER

INTO COMMUNION WITH THE ONE WHO IS

PRESENT TO US HERE AND NOW AND IS

THERE TO GIVE US

WHAT WE MOST NEED.

Henri Nouwen[2]

AT HOME IN THE CASTLE

• • •

OUR DESIRE TO PRAY HAS BECOME A

DOORWAY INTO THE HEART OF BEING.

Ann and Barry Ulanov[3]

Entering into prayer is like walking through a doorway to our soul, entering into the extraordinary by way of the ordinary, perhaps like Lucy and Edmund entered Narnia through the back of a wardrobe.[4] From the tasks of life that demand our time, energy, and attention, God's Spirit summons us to an inner chamber where a very present and available God awaits us. Distractions, busyness, people's needs, fatigue—all of these and more pull at us like poor beggars tugging at our sleeve with reasons we should attend to them instead: "Don't go! Don't leave me alone. There isn't time!" they cry.

Making time to be alone to pray is often the most challenging task we face all day. It's difficult for me, and my guess is that it may be hard for you sometimes too. In *The Interior Castle,* Teresa of Avila writes about a way she learned to pray meaningfully, to become receptive to and aware of Christ's presence as she met with him in prayer. She describes the soul as a castle. "We ourselves are the castle," says Teresa.[5] Isn't that a beautiful thought, our souls as hidden, interior castles in which we meet with Christ? This chapter explores the experience of being in relationship with Christ and particularly the role of stillness and solitude in our receptiveness to him.

Jesus said, "When you pray, go away by yourself, shut the door behind you, and pray to your Father secretly. Then your Father, who knows all secrets, will reward you" (Matthew 6:6, NLT).

In the secrecy of our interior castles, Christ ministers his presence to each of us, nurturing us, giving us what we need. The truths of his Word speak to us individually today just as they spoke to the disciples, whose temperaments, personalities, and vulnerabilities were as varied as those in any small group of men or women today. It came as no surprise to Jesus that Thomas struggled with doubt and asked to put his hand on Christ's wounded side before believing that Jesus was alive again after having been crucified. Nor was Jesus shocked by Peter's habit of popping off impulsively, promising more than he could deliver. In intimate, personal relationship with each of them, Jesus responded to their unique needs. In the same way, God wants us to meet him, to experience his presence, to know him and his truth—to be "at home" with him in our internal spiritual lives.

When I was in my early twenties, I lived in Germany for almost three years and once visited Neuschwanstein Castle (the "Disneyland" castle) in the northern region of the Bavarian Alps. Resplendent with rich, carved wood interiors and elegant paintings created for the pleasure of King Ludwig II, the castle was inhabited only a few months because Ludwig died shortly after the seventeen-year-long construction was completed. Though still filled with beautiful tapestries and furnishings, the castle felt cold and uninviting, like a decorated showplace nobody had ever felt "at home" in, which was exactly the case.

When we are still and silent in the interior castles of our souls, God meets us, restores us, reveals to us our "way of being" at that moment, and redirects and cleanses us. Through his presence and availability we become attuned to him the way a baby bonds with a nurturing mother. God's Word comes alive and speaks to us in the context of today's situation, weaving biblical truths into the fabric of our souls. It all happens in the context of relationship as we spend time being with God, getting to know him and being known by him.

ENGAGING IN RELATIONSHIP

• • •

THE BIBLICAL "KNOW" ALWAYS REFERS

TO AN INTIMATE, PERSONAL,

INTERACTIVE RELATIONSHIP.

Dallas Willard[6]

When I came to know Christ as a young adult, I began to study the Bible with some friends and to pray and worship with people in my church. I started learning the thoughts and ways of God by reading his Word, talking to him in prayer, and worshiping him as we sang hymns together in a church service, and sometimes I experienced God's presence in a moment of serendipitous wonder. But engaging in an intimate, personal, interactive relationship with Christ was something I began to know about gradually as I spent time alone with him. Relationships are fresh, vibrant, alive, changing, ever unfolding. We can enjoy them and experience their various aspects, but we cannot predict precisely how they will unfold. We see them unfold and grow as we spend time together.

It may help us to grasp the invisible reality of engaging in a spiritual relationship with Christ as we observe two people spending quality time together. One day I caught a glimpse of the power of someone's *being with* another person in, of all places, a session of play therapy.

Seven-year-old Lauren entered the playroom with her therapist as graduate students at the University of North Texas Center for Play Therapy observed from behind a two-way mirror. Lauren's eyes brightened as she looked around the room at walls lined with toy shelves, a sand tray, a well-stocked puppet cabinet, and a doll house. Her therapist smiled.

"What am I supposed to do?" asked Lauren.

"In the playroom you get to choose what to do," replied the play therapist.

Lauren began to twirl a lock of her long, straight brown hair around one finger and slowly walked over to the sand tray. Reaching to touch the golden grains, she looked back at the therapist for reassurance.

"You're not sure whether it's really okay to play in the sand," came the therapist's reflection. Lauren spread her fingers wide and raked her hand the full length of the tray, smiling as she savored the sensation of the tiny cool flecks of sand caressing her fingers. Then she dusted her hands off, walked over to the art table, and pulled up a chair.

"Now you're checking out the art supplies," said the play therapist, affirming acceptance of the child's choice. Without comment Lauren pulled a large sheet of manila paper from the table in front of her, picked up a blue crayon, and began to draw.

"This is my mom and dad," said Lauren, forming faces with detailed eyes, noses and mouths, arms, hands and feet; then she dumped the crayons from the box so she could see the colors more easily. As Lauren continued to draw, the therapist noticed her client had colored a boy with short black hair and a big smile. He was dressed in brown trousers and a red shirt. "Here's how my brother looks. I'm making everyone in my family," Lauren explained.

"So that's your brother, and now you're drawing yourself," said the therapist, aware that Lauren and her brother were the only children in the family.

"No, I'm there. I just don't show up," said Lauren.

A fleeting puzzled expression crossed the therapist's face.

"Nobody knows I'm there."

Momentary horror streaked across the therapist's face as she made a silent guess at what Lauren was communicating through words. Lauren tentatively looked up at the therapist as the sadness in her eyes bore confirmation of her words.

After a moment the therapist said reflectively, "Sometimes you feel invisible."

"Yes."

Has there ever been a time in your life with God, perhaps in the midst of a prayer in solitude, when you felt deeply known by him, the way Lauren sensed the play therapist's keen understanding of her? Far more capable of seeing to the bottom of our souls than any human being can do, God knows everything about us without our saying a word, yet he delights in our conversations with him, our trust, and the time we spend just being together with him. He wants to engage in intimate relationship with us.

In the final moment of the play therapy scene Lauren gave her therapist (and a room full of observing graduate students) a snapshot of her inner world and also engaged in a moment of intimate, personal, interactive relationship. Although the therapist had given little instruction or direction during her encounter with Lauren and had said little to her, something beyond description had happened during their time together: an exchange of awareness, sensitivity, understanding, and caring acceptance. Later that afternoon I read from the class text, *Play Therapy, The Art of the Relationship:* "Life cannot be described, it can only be experienced and appreciated. Descriptions can always be evaluated. Life cannot. Life is. It unfolds and is in totality at that moment, no more and no less."[7]

Young Lauren's encounter with the play therapist faintly hints at the Christian's experience of relationship with Christ—an intimate, personal, interactive encounter. *Being with* Christ in relationship transcends the elemental functions of what we think, do, and feel, just as the therapist's relationship with Lauren wasn't confined to the child's thoughts about the playroom supplies and rules, coloring and playing in the sand, or feeling insecure or curious. Their relationship was more about what happened when their eyes locked in a knowing gaze and acceptance and trust began to build as they spent time in each other's presence.

"Being" is like life—it just *is*. As we "be" with Christ (that is, engage with him) in prayer, we come to know him, trust him as our Lord, and find that we are fully accepted by him. In *The Shaking of the Foundations* German theologian Paul Tillich writes, "Do not seek for anything, do not perform anything, do not intend anything. Simply accept the fact that you are accepted."[8] To know that Christ accepts us in whatever state we are is to experience grace in our relationship with him in the same way that Lauren encountered the acceptance of the play therapist.

We prefer predictability, a guaranteed five-step plan for developing intimacy with God. But that's not the setup. "Follow me," Jesus said to those he was calling as disciples, "and I will make you fishers of men" (Matthew 4:19). *How will you lead me? Where will you send me? When will you do it?* they must have wondered, just as we do today. Our anxious demands only reveal the depth of our need to know and be known, moment to moment, by the great I AM, who simply *is*.

IN QUIETNESS, HE LEADS AND RESTORES US

• • •

GOD IS A PERSON, AND IN THE DEPTHS
OF HIS MIGHTY NATURE HE THINKS, WILLS,
ENJOYS, FEELS, LOVES, DESIRES AND SUFFERS
AS ANY OTHER PERSON MAY. GOD IS A PERSON
AND CAN BE KNOWN IN INCREASING DEGREES
OF INTIMACY AS WE PREPARE OUR HEARTS
FOR THE WONDER OF IT.

A. W. Tozer[9]

Do you ever wonder where those moments of peace in the green pastures, the tranquil walks beside still waters the psalmist spoke of can be found in your life, amidst the piles of laundry, trips to Wal-Mart, stacks of unfinished corporate reports, or week-to-week lesson plans? It's encouraging to remember that David, the psalmist, also had his hectic moments when he was running from enemies, planning battle strategies, and yearning for God's presence. "When can I go and meet with God?" he asked (Psalm 42:2).

How are we to find stillness and solitude in the midst of our busy lives? Henri Nouwen writes, "Solitude begins with a time and place for God, and him alone. If we really believe not only that God exists, but that he is actively present in our lives—healing, teaching, and guiding—we need to set aside a time and space to give him our undivided attention."[10] This may sound like an impossibility to you, especially if you are in the active phase of mothering years or working long hours at your job. It's not easy. But building persistence is one of the ways God strengthens our character. Some women I know get quite creative in finding ways to experience moments of solitude and stillness.

> Solitude begins with a time and place for God, and him alone. If we really believe not only that God exists, but that he is actively present in our lives—healing, teaching, and guiding—we need to set aside a time and space to give him our undivided attention.
>
> —Henri Nouwen, *Here and Now*

Vickie, a mom of four sons, two of whom were preschoolers at the time, longed for time to be with God, to think about the truths she'd read in her study that week, and to take a little time for prayer and enjoying a relationship with him. With her busy routine of homemaking and child rearing it wasn't easy to figure out how she might do that. After trying unsuccessfully to find ways to sandwich a prayer time between chores, children's naps, and cooking meals, she decided to hire a sitter two hours each week to free her for being with God and developing a relationship with him. Vickie had often hired someone to supervise her two younger sons during school hours when she went to lunch with a girlfriend. Yet she'd never thought of setting aside a little time and money just for being with God. It felt strange, like making an appointment with an invisible friend, and it took a commitment of time and money.

But the payoff was a small space of refreshment and rejuvenation in her week as she began to sense her knowledge of God growing deeper through the solitude and stillness she experienced with him. Gradually the time she spent alone developing a relationship with God began to influence more moments throughout her everyday routine as she experienced momentary reminders of his acceptance, presence, and availability. The leaves shaking in the breeze might offer a gentle reminder that God was with her as she took a walk with her children. An extra surge of patience during a tense moment of sibling rivalry might give her a glimpse of God's invisible support backing her up in her role as a mom, the way Lauren's eyes locked in a wordless compassionate gaze with those of the play therapist.

As you seek the heart of God, trust that he will nurture your soul with his truths and presence in ways unique to his relationship with you, ways that are respectful of your temperament, your life stage, and your personality. Because I spent so many years as a young Christian covering a lot of content in my prayers and Bible study, I like keeping things simple and slowed down in my spiritual life. Don't misunderstand: I believe we need to know what the Bible says and pray for the needs of others with some structure and regularity. But when it comes to being with Christ and enjoying my relationship with him, I like to savor the moments and keep things relatively unstructured rather than have a detailed agenda.

If you like the simple, slowed-down approach, try just sitting quietly and reminding yourself that you are with God at home in the interior castle of your soul. Let the noises around you fade into the background as you eagerly seek him (see Psalm 63:1). Trust that as you come near to God, he will come near to you (see James 4:8). Read a small portion of Scripture from your daily readings.

Read slowly; then pause and listen. You may hear a dog barking or a car door slamming in the street or voices from outside your house, but gently draw your attention back to the words of truth. Read the phrase again. Let the meaning of the words seep down past your intellect and into your heart. Can you picture this truth? Remind yourself again that you are with God. How does your body feel as you think about the words? Do your shoulders relax because the truth soothes you? Does your jaw tighten because you feel anxious about what you've read? What is God telling you about the state you are in right now as you sit with him?

Read, pause, listen. Does something jump out at you? You may want to write down some thoughts in a journal or spiral notebook as you reflect on what the words are saying to you. What response do you want to give? Taking a slow, deep drink of the Scriptures in the presence of God nurtures and cleanses the soul. As we continue to sit still and quiet with God, we may ask him to reveal to us the state of our soul in that moment as the psalmist did: "Search me, O God, and know my heart; test me and know my anxious thoughts. See if there is any offensive way in me, and lead me in the way everlasting" (Psalm 139:23-24).

During a conflict with her mother-in-law my friend Sue had a vague sense of inner unrest that kept her from feeling close to God. Unable to see past the smoke screen that was blocking her intimacy with him, Sue asked God to search her heart and reveal its contents, using the words from Psalm 139 above. For Sue and some other visual learners I have known, pictures come to mind before words do, so these people may engage in what has been called "snapshot journaling"; that is, rather than write out their thoughts during their time with God, they may instead sketch their impressions of what God is revealing to them in response to their prayer or reading. As Sue used colored pencils to sketch a stick figure with hands on her hips, a wide-open mouth with streaks of red coming out, and pointed brows over eyes narrowed into slits, the word jealous popped into her mind. The primitive drawing had revealed a snapshot of her interior life and something that was keeping her from intimacy in her relationship with God.

Yes, Sue admitted, *I am jealous of all the attention my mother-in-law is getting from my husband.* As Sue remained quiet and still in God's presence, he searched her heart and faithfully revealed something offensive in her soul at that moment. He instructed her through the truth of his Word, strengthened her to look at something undesirable in herself, and ministered compassionate forgiveness as she agreed with what he revealed. Sue might end her time of solitude by spending a few moments sorting out her thoughts and feelings prayerfully while relishing the comfort of God's accepting presence.

Another way to slow things down and savor your moments with God is to take a phrase from your daily reading and prayerfully repeat it several times, allowing time for reflection. In a talk author Jill Briscoe gave on the Twenty-third Psalm, she suggested that we approach God as a sheep feeding on his Word. "Have you ever watched sheep grazing in a field?" Jill asked. "They pull off a small clump of grass with their teeth, and then they begin to slowly chew. Then they chew, and chew, and chew, and chew. They chew all the goody out of the Word, like savoring the sweet out of a stick of gum."[11]

Jill also suggested concentrating on a short phrase from the Scriptures, saying the words slowly and emphasizing a different word each time you say it, allowing a few moments for reflection. Your exercise might look something like this:

"The Lord is my shepherd."

"The *Lord* is my shepherd." The Lord God, Creator of the universe, is my shepherd.

"The Lord *is* my shepherd." Here and now, in this time and place, he *is* my shepherd. Whatever may be happening to me cannot alter this truth.

"The Lord is *my* shepherd." The same Lord of Abraham and Isaac and Jacob and the psalmist is also *my* shepherd!

"The Lord is my *shepherd.*" The One whose voice I know, who comes looking for me when I fall into a hole or wander away to the other side of the hill, is my *shepherd.* He cares for me, carries me when I am weary, feeds me when I am hungry, and watches over me when I sleep.

I like Jill's suggestion of emphasizing one word at a time in a short phrase, and I have found it a helpful and peace-bringing practice. As we sit at the hearth of our interior castles, warming ourselves by the Fire and letting God's truth seep down past our intellects and into our hearts, God relieves our deepest loneliness. Slowed-down prayer and Bible reading become an interactive experience with our Lord, a setting for intimate relationship. He speaks to us; we listen; we say something to him. He speaks to us; we listen; we respond.

Then we go back into the busyness of our days taking a remnant of tranquillity with us. During the day, as we care for children, drive on a busy expressway, or perform the duties of our jobs, we can take a momentary break to remember the peace of being "at home" with God no matter what is happening around us. The taste of the "goody" we have chewed out of the Word has lingered with us for a little while.

PEACE—A GIFT FOR OTHERS

• • •

PEACE I LEAVE WITH YOU; MY PEACE
I GIVE YOU. I DO NOT GIVE TO YOU
AS THE WORLD GIVES. DO NOT LET
YOUR HEARTS BE TROUBLED
AND DO NOT BE AFRAID.

John 14:27

As we engage in intimate relationship with God, his presence sometimes evokes holy awe and wonder, just as the disciples in the boat were "in absolute awe, staggered." Recently I had to go into the hospital to have a minor procedure done. A couple of days before I was to be admitted, I was driving back to my office after preliminary lab work. As I passed by a large church in Dallas, I drove into the parking lot on a whim and decided to stop in for a brief time of prayer. I had only a few minutes, but I'd heard this church had a labyrinth, a path imprinted on the floor for people who wanted to pray as they walked. I really didn't know what to expect, or even what the labyrinth was, but because my mind was cluttered with fearful thoughts of the upcoming surgery, I hoped to find a few moments of peace there.

When I walked past the church foyer and arrived at the labyrinth, I noticed some printed directions at the starting place and picked up a copy to read. "The labyrinth has only one path, so there are no tricks to it and no dead ends. The path winds throughout and becomes a mirror for where we are in our spiritual lives; touches our sorrows and releases our joys. So walk it with an open mind and an open heart."

The words sounded vague, directionless, but I decided to just ask God to be with me in that moment and help me sense his presence as I walked. As I took a few steps on the path, I simply tried to remember that God was there with me, walking beside me, as he would be with me in the hospital in a couple of days. As I continued to walk, I noticed there was a kneeling bench in the center and mentally guessed the path must end there.

Soon I noticed I was mentally guessing which way the path would turn next, whether to the right or to the left. When I became aware that I was distracted, I drew my attention back to being alone with God here inside this church and inside my heart, where we were meeting together. At one point I came very near the center, and I thought the path was leading me to the kneeling bench, but then it took a sudden turn back to the outside of the circular path. Once again I drew my attention back to spending these moments alone with God. But the intrusive thoughts continued as I drew near the center again and then back to the outside of the circle.

Suddenly it occurred to me that this was the condition of my anxious heart. As I anticipated the medical procedure coming up, I was demanding to know what would happen, whether the procedure would achieve the hoped-for result or not. Realizing this, I began to just relax, keep walking, and forget the pattern of the twisting pathway. At last I arrived at the center and knelt at the bench. As I looked straight ahead, my eyes fell on a small cross encircled by a crown of thorns (it was the week before Easter), which stood in front of the window I'd passed as I entered the labyrinth. Until the moment when I knelt in the center, I had bypassed the cross, in fact, hadn't noticed it at all. Yet now as I took a few minutes to pray and just be with God, I was struck by its beauty, simplicity, the mystery I'd encountered, and the unexpected way God had met me to give me something I needed precisely at that moment.

As I finished the walk, left the church, and got into my car to drive back to the office, I knew I was better equipped to see the clients I had scheduled that afternoon, to set aside the urgency of my own concerns and meet them where they were. My brief time alone with God had encouraged and strengthened me and renewed my hope.

Ultimately, what we experience in stillness and solitude with God are gifts for us to share with other people around us. We are not here to just be sitting still, feeling peaceful all the time. We are here to be in the storms of life—our own and those of other people. But if there have been no times when we have been alone and silent, finding restoration in Christ's presence, we cannot offer others anything of substance; we have only ripples to add to the whirlwinds of their lives.

Most of the time we are not aware of the ways our being "at home" with Christ in our internal spiritual lives benefits others or how our prayers may change things in other people's lives, but they do have an effect.

I heard a moving story about a man named Staretz Silouan, a poor and simple Russian peasant whose solitude and prayers drastically altered the quality of life and the futures of people who worked under his direction. He went to Mount Athos, a holy mount in Greece where monasteries, hermitages, and cloisters are completely dedicated to prayer and worship of God. Silouan made his journey to Athos as a young man in his twenties and ended

up staying about fifty years, supervising some of the workers who came to the monastery to make a little money in
hopes of returning to their villages to start a family. Other
monks in charge of workshops had trouble with their
workers, who tried to cheat and deceive them, and they
observed how those under Staretz Silouan's supervision
worked diligently without much direction. Curious, they
asked how he managed this.

"I don't know," Father Silouan replied, explaining
that he always prayed compassionately for them before
coming to the workshop in the mornings. He then gave
them the task they were to perform during the day, telling
them that as long as they would work, he would pray about
each of them individually. His prayers went something like
this: "O Lord, remember Nicholas. He is young, he is just
twenty, he has left in his village his wife, who is even younger than he, and their first child. Can you imagine the
misery there is there that he has had to leave them because
they could not survive on his work at home. Protect them
in his absence. Shield them against every evil. Give him
courage to struggle through this year and go back to the joy
of a meeting, with enough money, but also enough courage to face the difficulties."

Father Silouan said he initially prayed with tears of
compassion for Nicholas, for his young wife, for the little
child. But as he was praying, the sense of God's presence
began to grow on him and "at a certain moment it grew so
powerful that I lost sight of Nicholas, his wife, his child,
his needs, their village, and I could be aware only of God,
and I was drawn by the sense of the divine presence deeper
and deeper, until of a sudden, at the heart of this presence, I met the divine love holding Nicholas, his wife, and
his child, and now it was with the love of God that I began
to pray for them again."

So it went with Father Silouan's days as he prayed for
each of the men under his supervision, one after another.
"When the day is over I go, I say a few words to them, we
pray together and they go to their rest."[12] Engaged in compassionate prayer as he encountered the presence of God,

Staretz Silouan's prayers in stillness and solitude changed the lives of those around him.

We don't have to go and stay in a monastery to pray fervently for others or to cultivate a deep, meaningful relationship with God. The difficult thing is finding moments to be still and silent so that we can be restored, redirected, and renewed as we spend time in God's presence. In the context of caring, interactive relationship with our Lord, he changes us and gives us something to pass on to others—his peace. He beckons us to return often to the interior castle, where we feel most at home. As Thomas à Kempis said, "The more you visit, the more you will want to return."[13]

• • •

AND SO IT IS: GOD CALLS US—

SEEKING US TO SEEK HIM—AND

OUR HEARTS RESONATE WITH

LONGING FOR HIM.

David Roper[14]

CRYING OUT ALONE
IN A DARK WOOD

Discovering God's Presence When He Seems Absent

• • •

SOME COME, NOT SO MANY ANY MORE BUT
ALWAYS SOME, ALWAYS ENOUGH, AND THE LORD
KNOWS WHY THEY DO, WHY WE DO. PROBABLY
FOR THE SAME REASON THAT FOR CENTURY
AFTER CENTURY MEN HAVE ALWAYS COME — BECAUSE
ALTHOUGH THERE IS MUCH THAT WE CANNOT
UNDERSTAND, MUCH THAT WE CANNOT BELIEVE,
THE INEXORABLE LIFE IN HIM DRAWS US TO HIM
THE WAY A GLIMMER OF LIGHT DRAWS A MAN
WHO HAS LOST HIS WAY IN THE DARK.

Frederick Buechner[1]

One Sunday in church the pastor announced that we would be seeing a film. Frank looked at me and shrugged just before the lights went out. In the film, chosen to help illustrate the pastor's point for the day, a mountain lion chased a defenseless bear cub out onto a fragile tree over-hanging a rushing river. As the big cat closed in on the whimpering cub, it began batting and bloodying the little bear's muzzle. It looked like a sure end for the baby bear, and I noticed the people in front of us fidgeting in their seats and wringing their hands, as I was. "Help! Help!" we wanted to cry out on the defenseless cub's behalf. Where was his mother, anyway?

Just as the mountain lion was about to go in for the kill, Mama Bear approached from behind her cub, reared up on her hind legs, and let out a ferocious roar. *Yes! Mama to the rescue! And not a moment too soon!* The cat turned to run as viewers let out a sigh of relief.

As the film ended and the lights came on, I scanned the congregation and saw mothers hugging daughters, wives putting their arms around their husbands, and Frank gave my hand a squeeze. I knew a couple of my friends were going through trying times and were feeling out on a limb, abandoned by God, and probably barely able to drag themselves to church that day. During the previous week we had learned of a husband's three-year affair and a child who had suddenly been stricken with an unidentified illness. Somehow this brief film had reassured many of us that in our darkest hours when we need God most and can't understand why he doesn't help us or answer our calls, he's somewhere out there beyond the range of our vision, rearing up and growling at the evils in our lives in ways we'll never be aware of.

In our darkest hours when we need God most and can't understand why he doesn't help us or answer our calls, he's somewhere out there beyond the range of our vision, rearing up and growling at the evils in our lives in ways we'll never be aware of.

Sooner or later if we live long enough, we come to a place in our spiritual journey where our life with God turns dark, dry, barren. We feel as if he has abandoned us and left us defenseless against enemies threatening to devour us. In these dark times there are no spiritual cookie crumbs marking a sure path home through the forest. There is no bright moon glistening overhead to light the way for us as it did for Hansel and Gretel. We call out to God to save us from the bubbling cauldrons waiting to boil us alive, and God does not answer. We get no assurances of answered prayer, no signs of God's caring, no warm affirmations of his presence. There is only the desire for God as we grope for him in the darkness.

When Job felt abandoned by God, he cried out desperately to him in these words: "Surely no one lays a hand on a broken man when he cries for help in his distress. Have I not wept for those in trouble? Has not my soul grieved for the poor? Yet when I hoped for good, evil came; when I looked for light, then came darkness" (Job 30:24-26). Like Job, when we feel alone in the dark, it seems that God gives us exactly what we *don't* need, ask for, or what's good for us. We call out, straining to hear that still, whispering Voice that was once so present. But the only answer we hear, if we hear anything at all, is the echo of our own voice.

> *Do you ever feel alone, in the dark,*
> *Like a child in an abandoned house at midnight?*
> *Do you cry out in the darkness, "Is anybody home?"*
> *And all that answers is your echo, "Is anybody home?"*
> *And you feel your way along the wall*
> *Hoping to find a doorway.*
> *"Hello?" you call out.*
> *"Hello?" your voice echoes,*
> *"Is anybody home?"*
> *And you feel alone—all alone.*
> *In the darkness you cry out,*
> *"Where are You, God?*
> *Why did You abandon me?"*
> *And you hear a faint echo . . .*
> *Somewhere, in the distance,*
> *Where a perfect man cries out*
> *From a cross on a hill,*
> *"Why did you abandon me, O God?"*

And then you know you're not alone.
It is dark. But you're not alone.

In darkness, even our Lord Jesus Christ once had to experience the absence of God. So it's not likely we'll get out of it. Just as the Crucifixion had to come before the Resurrection, darkness must come before morning's first light. When we are feeling most abandoned by God, we are really not alone but perhaps most present with God.

John of the Cross is known for writing the classic treatise *Dark Night of the Soul,* in which he describes periods when the soul learns to love God for the sake of God himself instead of for any personal rewards of the experience of knowing him and belonging to him: "Herein God secretly teaches the soul and instructs it in perfection of love, without its doing anything."[2]

God decides how long the season of spiritual darkness will last, how many turns our path through the forest will take. The gospel truths never change, but by the time they get thoroughly mixed in with our messy variations on humanity, our lives are never going to turn out as the neat, predictable stories that read the same every time, like *Hansel and Gretel.* In the Meantime, our path through a dark wood leads to a clearing lying just beyond our sight, knowledge, or understanding.

HOPE IS BIRTHED IN DARKNESS

• • •

UNTO THIS DARKNESS WHICH IS BEYOND
LIGHT WE PRAY THAT WE MAY COME, AND
THROUGH LOSS OF SIGHT AND KNOWLEDGE
MAY SEE AND KNOW THAT WHICH TRANSCENDS
SIGHT AND KNOWLEDGE, BY THE VERY FACT
THAT NOT SEEING AND KNOWING; FOR THIS
IS REAL SIGHT AND KNOWLEDGE.

Dionysius, Sixth-Century Mystic[3]

Every year just before Thanksgiving Frank plants an amaryllis bulb. Within days a green shoot breaks through the soil and begins to grow rapidly. By Christmas Day a beautiful cluster of brightly colored trumpets has burst forth from the top of the tall, strawlike stalks, heralding hope born from beneath the soil's dark surface. Frank usually buys the bulb in a kit at Home Depot or Kmart. But last year he decided to keep the bulb after the flower had withered and save it for the next growing season.

"The bulb must be protected from freezing and put away in a dark, dry place for storage," Frank explained to me. "If you look at it during dormancy, it appears dried up and dead, ready to be thrown into the trash. During this time, the bulb is waiting for its next flowering season."

Awaiting a time when it will again be nestled into loose, warm soil and begin reaching for the sun, the dried amaryllis bulb shows no visible sign of the magic of photosynthesis to come, when it will again be nurtured and begin reaching upward. Yet in a way only God understands, living color has been stored up during the period of darkness and dormancy.

Like the amaryllis, when we experience a season of dried-up spiritual life, nothing consoles us. We're not aware that anything productive is happening. We may feel useless, indifferent, trapped in the dark desperation of our loneliness. Or maybe we feel nothing. Yet during this time of dormancy, whatever it is we will next need is being stored up for a season we as yet know nothing about.

Sometimes when we are waiting in the darkness, hope keeps us going as we envision something better ahead. In the haunting movie *The Shawshank Redemption*, Andy Dufresne is convicted of killing his wife and sentenced to life at Shawshank Prison. He meets up with Red, the contact man who can get inmates anything they want from the outside. Together and separately Andy and Red endure untold horrors.

Andy is not a typical inmate. He wins the trust of his superiors, and before long he's running the prison library and keeping financial records for the warden. But Andy spends his spare hours quietly, alone in his cell. Concealed behind a large Rita Hayworth poster, he tediously picks his way through the crumbling cement sequestering the prison in his attempt to tunnel his way to the outside. Throughout his years at Shawshank, the poster of the movie star changes with the times, but Andy held an unchanging vision in his heart of where he would go if he ever got out. That vision is what kept Andy going through a long period of darkness, and it is what eventually got him from prison to the coast of Mexico, where he is shown on the beach in a final scene of the movie.

Like Andy, sometimes we hang on to hope through a dark time by envisioning a better day ahead. From a Christian perspective, if anyone should be able to cling to hope in the darkness, we should. We may remind ourselves of this and seek confirmation in the Scriptures, yet the verses we find seem to affirm only that we must be off track because we're not encouraged. And still the pitch black darkness hovers, quiet, still, ominous. We wait. We strain to hear. We squint into the darkness but see nothing. We don't understand God's takeoffs on photosynthesis.

Reaching beyond Our Own Darkness

Christine was a single woman who once dreamed of finding "Mr. Right" and raising a Christian family. Now in her late thirties, she had gone to night classes to earn her MBA and had worked her way up the corporate ladder to the position of senior budget analyst. She'd bought a house, saved some money, joined a Christian singles group, and kept praying that God would send that special someone for her to share her life with. Although Christine was attractive, sincere, capable, and lots of fun, she'd never had a long-term relationship with a man.

At this midlife stage and nearing the end of her child-bearing years, Christine became depressed and felt sad and lonely even though nothing had changed in her routine. She found it increasingly difficult to concentrate at her job or to get a good night's sleep. "My life feels totally meaningless," she said. "I'm trying to hang on to truth, and I know all of God's promises, but they're not ringing true for me! I've prayed for years just like Suzanne and Kathy (two friends from their singles group who had recently married), but now my heart just aches. Does God even care?"

Christine described her loneliness, the indifference she perceived when she explained her hurt to some women in their group who had met somebody to either date or marry. Other friends appeared content with single life, even welcoming the free time with fewer demands on their energy. But Christine's desire for a family would not go away. Her parents and sister lived in another state, which made it impossible for her to visit except for holidays.

The fog of gloom hovering over Christine seemed impenetrable, though friends stopped by the house more frequently to check on her and her supervisor allowed more flexibility in her work schedule. But soon Christine started missing more days at work and staying in bed until noon on Saturdays. Finally Christine's doctor suggested that she take a leave of absence from her job. A friend helped her get her house ready for a six-month lease and helped her pack up for a long visit with her sister in Maryland.

About a year later I ran into Christine at a seminar we both attended. She explained that renewing ties with her family had helped, but even with added support from loved ones, she had still felt as if God had turned his back on her. They'd had some adventures and made a trip to Washington, D.C. Then one Sunday Christine and her sister were dressing in preparation for a visit to a large church in Baltimore where an organ soloist was scheduled to play during the service. As Christine glanced out the window, her attention was captured by a clump of bright yellow flowers growing at the base of a small tree. The flowers had been there all along, but today when Christine looked at them, the petals seemed to shine more brightly. The fresh dewdrops glistened in the sunshine, and her heart felt a little lighter. For the first time in many months Christine hoped the gloomy darkness of her mood was beginning to lift.

It was to be a day of adventure, beginning with some

inspiring music. After the service was over, a few people had gone to the front of the church for prayer, where the pastor had invited them to come and kneel at an altar. Christine lingered to watch and was struck by an unexpected insight. As the pastor approached those kneeling at the altar, each person whispered his or her request in his ear. He softly prayed for that request and ended by saying, "Bless you." Then he moved on, touching each person gently on the shoulder as he prayed.

Christine was intrigued when she noticed that as the pastor finished praying for one person, that one would rise and stand behind the next person being prayed for, also gently placing a hand on his or her shoulder. Soon a line began to form behind the person being prayed for as the pastor moved slowly from one side of the altar to the other. Each time, another person joined the line and touched the shoulder of the one in front.

As Christine watched people kneeling to be prayed for and then getting up and moving to touch someone else, she suddenly realized that she no longer felt alone in her sense of isolation and emptiness. Her pain over not finding the right person to marry and the loneliness she experienced living as a single person was one version of human pain—part of the greater pain of humanity, which all people share in different ways.

Soon Christine returned to Dallas, moved back into her house, and resumed her job, with some broader perspectives than she'd had when she went to Maryland to visit her sister. She now had a desire to care for other people beyond what they could give her, to reach out to others in their unspoken pain and unmet needs, which she realized were a part of each human being even when people didn't talk about them. Nothing magical had happened. The period of darkness had come to an end in God's time. Christine had been given a larger vision for loving people, a desire to love God for his own sake. It didn't mean that her desire for a husband went away—it didn't. But Christine emerged from the darkness wiser, more patient, and more genuine than she was before.

As the gloom lifted, God's presence shone through a time when he had seemed absent. Listen to these words from Frederick Buechner: "The preacher tells the truth by speaking of the visible absence of God because if he doesn't see and own up to the absence of God in the world, then he is the only one there who doesn't see it, and who then is going to take him seriously when he tries to make real what he claims also to see as the invisible presence of God in the world?"[4]

Perhaps you've entered a dark season in your spiritual life and you are groping for God, feeling your way, hoping for a glimmer of light. All of us will face a time of crying out in desperation when God seems absent. At such times he is not doing *nothing*. He is tunneling, digging deeper, storing up, broadening, stretching us in ways we cannot see. We are "morphing," turning from a worm into a butterfly. It is in these times that Hannah's song is written. Moses' weakness is being turned into strength. Something transcendent to our knowledge and awareness is happening. Sometimes the thing we're trying so hard to escape from in the dark turns out to be the very thing that protects us.

In C. S. Lewis's *The Horse and His Boy*, book 5 in the Chronicles of Narnia series, a boy named Shasta describes for us all what it's like to feel alone in the dark, far from safety, comfort, good fortune, and how it is that at such times God is truly most with us.

Shasta and a talking horse named Bree had made their way to the northern country called Narnia, where life promised to be better. Shasta had never known his real father or mother and had been brought up by a stern fisherman. At the first chance, he had run away, but alas, now he was lost in a dark wood. He wasn't used to mountain country, so he didn't realize he was perhaps right at the top of the pass that led from Archenland to Narnia.

Shasta thought he must be the most unfortunate boy that ever lived. It seemed to him that everything went right for everyone except him; that all the others traveling before him must have arrived safely at their destination except him. Now Shasta was tired, cold, and hungry, and tears began to roll down his face.

But he was suddenly frightened when he heard someone walking beside him. It was pitch dark, so he could not see anything, but Shasta got the impression it was a very large creature, and he bit his lip in terror. Then he hoped he was only imagining that something or someone was there. At last Shasta could bear the suspense no longer:

"Who are you?" he said, scarcely above a whisper.

"One who has waited long for you to speak," said the Thing. . . . "Tell me your sorrows."

Shasta was a little reassured by [the Thing's warm breath]: so . . . he told the story of his escape and how they were chased by lions and forced to swim for their lives . . . and also, how very long it was since he had had anything to eat.

"I do not call you unfortunate," said the Thing.

"Don't you think it was bad luck to meet so many lions?" said Shasta.

"There was only one lion," said the Voice.

"What on earth do you mean? I've just told you there were at least two the first night, and—"

"There was only one: but he was swift of foot."

"How do you know?"

"I was the lion." And as Shasta gaped with open mouth and said nothing, the Voice continued. . . . "I was the lion who drove the jackals from you while you slept. I was the lion who gave the Horses the new strength of fear for the last mile. . . . And I was the lion you do not remember who pushed the boat in which you lay, a child near death, so that it came to shore where a man sat, wakeful at midnight, to receive you." . . .

The mist was turning from black to gray and from gray to white. This must have begun to happen some time ago, but while he had been talking to the Thing he had not been noticing anything

else. . . . He turned and saw, pacing beside him
. . . a lion. . . . After one glance at the Lion's
face, he slipped out of the saddle and fell at its
feet. He couldn't say anything but then he didn't
want to say anything, and he knew he needn't say
anything. . . .

"I see," said Shasta to himself. "Those are the
big mountains between Archenland and Narnia.
I was on the other side of them yesterday. I must
have come through the pass in the night. What
luck that I hit it!—at least it wasn't luck at all
really, it was Him. And now I'm in Narnia."[5]

In the end Shasta rejoins his friends and his real father—
the king—and lives happily in the land of Narnia.

Like Shasta, as we feel our way along the edge of life's
cliffs in the dark, we are not alone. Even when we feel
abandoned, left out, cruelly treated, God is beside us,
guiding us through narrow passes and guarding us through
untold harm.

Hello?

Is anybody home?

Shhhh. Hope is being birthed. Morning's light is on the
way.

• • •

STRENGTHEN THOSE WHO HAVE TIRED HANDS,

AND ENCOURAGE THOSE WHO HAVE WEAK KNEES.

SAY TO THOSE WHO ARE AFRAID, "BE STRONG, AND

DO NOT FEAR, FOR YOUR GOD IS COMING

TO DESTROY YOUR ENEMIES. HE IS

COMING TO SAVE YOU."

Isaiah 35:3-4, NLT

SITTING IN THE KING'S LAP

Learning to Practice the Presence of God

• • •

THERE IS NO EVENT SO COMMONPLACE

BUT THAT GOD IS PRESENT WITHIN IT,

ALWAYS HIDDENLY, ALWAYS LEAVING YOU

ROOM TO RECOGNIZE HIM OR NOT TO RECOGNIZE

HIM, BUT ALL THE MORE FASCINATINGLY BECAUSE

OF THAT, ALL THE MORE COMPELLINGLY

AND HAUNTINGLY.

Frederick Buechner[1]

One day our friend Lynn phoned to invite Frank and me to her home the next evening for dinner and a time of prayer. "Brad and I just want to have a few friends over to be together in God's presence and pray for an hour," Lynn said, naming about six other friends who would also be coming and who had been gathering like this for a number of weeks. "You can pray silently or aloud, for personal or national concerns or whatever you choose, it makes no difference." Frank and I talked it over and decided to go, partly because Brad and Lynn were interesting people and we wanted to get to know them better and partly because the simplicity of the invitation was appealing—just come, eat, and pray comfortably with friends.

As we pulled up in front of their house the next evening, other guests had already arrived. Brad had just finished grilling pork chops; Lynn was putting homemade
cheese biscuits into the oven, and their daughters were
skipping up and down the stairs. Soon we sat down to a
delicious dinner, two more guests arrived, and we enjoyed
a leisurely conversation. After the table was cleared, the
adults retired to the living room, and the children were
instructed to play upstairs. We admired the oil paintings
hanging on the walls and learned Lynn had painted them
herself and often sold her work in galleries. She lit candles
on the coffee table and dimmed the overhead lights, and
we all settled in our chairs to begin the prayer time.

"Instead of taking time to share requests, let's just pray
for what's on our hearts," Brad said. So began a sweet and
memorable hour around God's throne with these new
friends in various stages of life—two married couples, one
single mom, and two young men in college. As we closed
our eyes, the distant chatter of children's voices in the
background mingled with ours as some made brief
requests on behalf of a family member and others gave
thanks for renewed health or just remained silent. Once
or twice I heard Lynn whispering to her daughter Emily,
who had come downstairs to ask a question.

At one point near the end of our prayer time, Lynn sat
beside me passionately pouring out her deep concern for
the state of our nation following the terrorist onslaught of
9/11. On my other side Brad had begun to snore, softly at
first, but gradually the sound grew loud enough that Lynn
interrupted her prayer. "Brad," she whispered. "Brad!
You're snoring!" Brad looked up, perhaps a bit embarrassed as some of us opened our eyes and giggled. He
shifted his weight in the soft chair, and we all closed our
eyes again as Lynn resumed her prayer.

Although I no longer recall much about the content of
our prayers that evening, what sticks in my memory is the
experience of being comfortable together and feeling safe
as we prayed, like children gathered on the ample lap of a
wise and gracious parent or grandparent. It didn't make

any difference if someone went to sleep or there were interruptions or noise in the background or whether we were silent or vocal. We were at peace with ourselves and each other in God's presence.

Perhaps it takes some years of walking with God to learn to relax in his presence, to realize that he's there even when he seems absent, and that he's not put off when we get distracted from him or go to sleep in his lap. He isn't even shocked at our worst foibles and follies, though we often are. Like a weaned child resting against its mother's breast, we stop thrashing about, demanding blessing on our terms, and begin to find contentment in trusting God—his character and grace. In her book *Gift from the Sea,* Anne Morrow Lindbergh speaks of her desire to live "in grace" as much of the time as possible: "I believe most people are aware of periods in their lives when they seem to be 'in grace' and other periods when they feel 'out of grace.' . . . In the first happy condition, one seems to carry all one's tasks before one lightly, as if borne along on a great tide; and in the opposite state one can hardly tie a shoe-string. It is true that a large part of life consists in learning a technique of tying the shoe-string, whether one is in grace or not. But there are techniques of living too; there are even techniques in the search for grace. And techniques can be cultivated."[2]

> Perhaps it takes some years of walking with God to learn to relax in his presence, to realize that he's there even when he seems absent and that he's not put off when we get distracted from him or go to sleep in his lap. He isn't even shocked at our worst foibles and follies, though we often are.

What "techniques" are you cultivating or would you like to cultivate so that you can live comfortably in God's presence in your everyday life? Jesus said, "Walk with me and work with me—watch how I do it. Learn the unforced rhythms of grace. I won't lay anything heavy or ill-fitting on you. Keep company with me and you'll learn to live freely and lightly" (Matthew 11:29-30, *THE MESSAGE*). Finding an unforced pattern and rhythm for living comfortably with God as we work, play, and interact with others revolves around watching for him, walking and working with Christ through everyday moments, and finding our fitting way of doing it.

The seventeenth-century French Carmelite Nicholas Herman, who came to be known as Brother Lawrence, called this "the practice of the presence of God" in his well-known book by that title. Like us, it took a while for Brother Lawrence to find a fitting way of walking with God. At eighteen he became a soldier and fought in the Thirty Years' War. But he was wounded and sent home, which ended his military career.

Haunted by recurring memories of the war's atrocities, Brother Lawrence was driven to devote his life to Christ in a more concrete way. He tried working for the treasurer of the king of France, but that didn't work because he was clumsy and kept breaking things. Next he met a wealthy man who had given up everything to become a hermit, and Brother Lawrence decided he would try this too, but life as a hermit only confused him. Then he decided he needed to belong to a religious community that would help to give his spiritual life some kind of pattern.

At last he became a brother at a Carmelite monastery and was given the job of working in the kitchen, where he served many years, and later in the shoe repair shop when a bad leg confined him to a sitting-down job.[3] He writes of concentrating on being aware of God's holy presence as he went about his everyday tasks: "I concentrate on being always in His holy presence. I keep myself there by simply paying attention and gazing lovingly at God . . . a habitual, silent, and secret conversation between the soul and God."[4]

Brother Lawrence explained that sometimes his thoughts wandered because he had to pay attention to something else or because of his own weakness, but then, he says, "I am soon reminded by inward feelings so delightful and delicious that I am embarrassed to talk about them."[5] As for sin, when he failed, he simply admitted it, saying, "I will always fail if you leave me on my own; it is up to you to keep me from falling and heal what is wrong with me."[6]

It wasn't the fulfillment of the work Brother Lawrence did that made him joyful but the practice of concentrating on God as he did it, drawing his attention back to Christ as he went about his daily routine and tasks in a fitting environment. He had to rule out some occupations and settings because they left him alone too much or didn't lend enough structure to his life to help him thrive or because he didn't have the right skills to perform those tasks. He had to try a few different environments before he found something that "fit" his temperament, gifts, limitations, and needs for emotional security and stability.

WATCHING AND LISTENING FOR GOD

• • •

THESE WORDS THAT GOD SPEAKS TO US . . . ARE

NOT MIRACLES THAT CREATE FAITH

AS WE MIGHT THINK THAT A MESSAGE WRITTEN

IN THE STARS WOULD CREATE, BUT THEY

ARE MIRACLES THAT IT TAKES FAITH TO SEE—

FAITH IN THE SENSE OF OPENNESS, FAITH IN THE

SENSE OF WILLINGNESS TO WAIT, TO WATCH,

TO LISTEN, FOR THE INCREDIBLE PRESENCE

OF GOD HERE IN THE WORLD AMONG US.

Frederick Buechner[7]

For those living "in grace," practicing God's presence doesn't happen in exactly the same way for everyone. It's not something exclusive that young moms, social workers, or dental assistants can't enter into. Everyone is invited to live in the lap of God's grace. As we become aware of what keeps us there, we should intentionally hold on to our valuable

Everyone is invited to live in the lap of God's grace.

finds or discoveries, making a collection and weaving a way of life from them the same way birds gather strands of berry skins and twigs from their environment to make their nests.

When Frank and I were living in the country, I once made a collection of abandoned bird nests. Perhaps it was symbolic of my life stage as I passed from active mothering to the slower pace of the empty nest. One of the nests was light and airy, shallow, loosely woven, and laced with pieces of dried snakeskin and little bits of insulation Frank had used as he built our house. Another was quite heavy—a deep, sturdy clump of leaf skeletons and mud tightly packed together—and still another, a tidy weaving of twigs, threads, and squirrel fur. Each nest reflected something of the bird's environment and what was available for gathering near its homing space.

The same is true for us: the things we need in order to live "in grace" vary depending on our temperaments, schedules, energy levels, stage of life, resources, and other variables surrounding our lives. We're all put together a little differently. In Matthew 13 the disciples asked Jesus why he used parables to explain the mysteries of the kingdom to the multitudes. He replied, "to create readiness, to nudge the people toward receptive insight. In their present state they [the multitudes] can stare till doomsday and not see it, listen till they're blue in the face and not get it" (v. 13, *THE MESSAGE*). Jesus taught people hidden truths through the mysteries of the mundane—planting seeds on different kinds of ground, tares and treasure in a field, a woman hiding leaven in a batch of meal.

Sometimes we miss the ways of paying attention to God that are right before our eyes: through our everyday tasks and routines. Living "freely and lightly" in God's presence will fit with our immediate environment and familiar surroundings. If you're a young mother, you are in the company of little psalmists! Children are natural seers—they have no problem imagining the mountains bowing down and the trees clapping as they rejoice at the sound of Jesus' name.

Of course you'll need breaks from them at times. But you don't have to get away from children to "practice the presence" of God. In fact, little people with fresh minds and untamed responses to life have a lot to teach us grown-ups about seeing God throughout our days.

"Hello?" a young voice answered when I dialed up the Roszhart residence.

"Hi, Naomi, this is Mrs. Waggoner."

"I thought so," said Naomi. "Do you want to talk to my mom?" While I had called to speak to Naomi's mom, Linda, I didn't want to miss a chance for a few words with a delightful eight-year-old.

"In a minute. But first, tell me what you've been doing today."

"Oh, not much."

"Really? What did you do this morning?"

"Oh, we just went to Wal-Mart to get a birthday present, and then I had gymnastics."

"Well, you had a pretty busy morning then?"

"And after lunch we went swimming, and now we're getting ready to eat Popsicles."

Then mom took over the Roszhart end of the conversation. "Yes, it's just been a typically uneventful day around here," she said as we both laughed.

Linda has a busy life filled with the joys and demands of child raising—home school, carpooling, dance lessons, cooking, and family life. With relatives living in the neighborhood and frequent visits from parents and in-laws, the Roszhart household is always abuzz. Yet Linda is one of those people who "carries her tasks lightly." She laughs a lot, makes time for friends as her schedule allows, brings joy to others, and enjoys the simple pleasures of life.

I've never heard Linda describe her way of "paying attention and gazing lovingly" at God as Brother Lawrence described, but it's apparent that she has found ways to practice his presence in her life. Seeing God through the small pairs of eyes right in front of her—her children's—is one way of cooperating with her busy life stage and style instead of waiting to "get spiritual" after her little girls grow up.

Once Frank and I were invited out to the Roszharts' plot of land to "survey it" before they began construction of their new home. As we adults talked about the positioning of the house and garage among the trees, Naomi, Rebecca, and Emily roamed the woods in search of critter friends and treasures to collect from mud puddles and under large rocks. Rebecca proudly presented a hand-picked weed flower to Linda. "Here! This is for you, Mommy!" she said.

"Oh, thank you, Rebecca." Linda took time to look her child in the eye and savor the joy of that moment, delighting in her devoted daughter's company. One of my greatest joys as Linda's friend is catching vicarious glimpses of God's wonders through her children's questions and observations of his ways and presence in nature: "Why do ants crawl along a sidewalk in a straight line but geese fly in a V?" "Do ants have chins?" Ah yes, we can learn much from these young contemplatives.

Linda is a reflective person by nature. She and I once enjoyed reading the same books and then getting together weekly to share our thoughts, personal applications, and questions with each other. During those days our schedules were not so full, and we lived closer. Occasionally we still meet at Applebee's to talk without interruptions. We talk about ways we've been seeing God in our lives and in people around us, how we've been distracted and weak and failed God and others.

Linda gets together with a group of girlfriends for a dinner club once a month and takes her daughters to a "mother's day out" once a week. This gives some built-in breaks from child care and other home responsibilities, which is the environment where her service is concentrated at this stage of her life. She would be the first to admit that she gets frustrated from time to time with the limitations of her routine as she longs for more time to be still, quiet, and practice God's presence with fewer distractions. Still, instead of working against the natural flow of her life at this stage, she cultivates techniques that allow her to live "in grace" here and now rather than wait till a decade down the road.

• • •

BUT YOU HAVE GOD-BLESSED EYES—

EYES THAT SEE! AND GOD-BLESSED EARS—

EARS THAT HEAR!

Matthew 13:16, *THE MESSAGE*

FINDING THE SLIPPER THAT FITS

• • •

I WILL WALK AMONG YOU;

I WILL BE YOUR GOD,

AND YOU WILL BE MY PEOPLE.

Leviticus 26:12, NLT

Perhaps you've tried to walk closely with God but were cultivating techniques that didn't really fit for you. Just like Cinderella's perfectly-fitting glass slipper, they appeared to fit beautifully for a mentor or friend, someone you admired, but the same way of "concentrating on God" felt forced when you tried it. Cramming ourselves into someone else's spiritual mold is like putting our feet into someone else's comfortably worn shoes—it feels unnatural. It doesn't fit. As we seek a comfortable, "free and light" way of serving God and practicing his presence while accepting our own strengths and limitations as Brother Lawrence did, God will unfold our way before us.

My friend Guianna is a genuine Proverbs 31 woman. She clearly serves Christ by serving others, concentrating on God through actions and good deeds rather than through words, thoughts, or reflections. She rises early in the morning, sees to the needs of her household, takes care of the practical needs of her family by cooking meals and canning vegetables her husband brings in from the garden. She often travels to Louisiana to visit her handicapped brother and gives high priority to helping family friends in need. I still recall her caring phone calls, visits, tasty casseroles, and desserts she brought to our house after I had major surgery. She followed up the next week as a mobile bed-and-breakfast service, showing up at our house to fix breakfast as I lay in bed recovering.

The rhythm of Guianna's "free and light" walk with God follows a well-ordered pattern of service—this fits for her. Guianna doesn't like drawing attention to herself, and I've never heard her speak of talking to God throughout the day or "paying attention" to him. She simply personifies the servant traits of Christ without appearing to even think about it. She finds fulfillment by quietly pleasing God in practical, substantive ways.

But maybe you're not like my friend Guianna. The Proverbs 31 model of Christian servanthood doesn't fit for everyone. As I've discussed earlier, when I was a young Christian, I somehow got the idea that this was *the* biblical model all Christian women were supposed to follow if they wanted to walk closely with God. It was also the model highly esteemed in the church I was a part of at that time. But when I tried taking meals to moms with newborn babies and so centering my fulfillment on regularly performed tasks and meeting the practical needs of others (and I did, for over a decade), it felt as if I was just playing a role, mechanically doing good deeds in hopes of earning love instead of serving others from my heart.

Although I was trying to "concentrate on God" in my prayers, I was really concentrating more on *me* than on him. *Was I doing okay? Had I been good enough, done enough, learned enough?* I self-consciously compared myself to women who embodied servant traits I admired and tried to force on myself, but the pattern didn't fit for me. Eventually I ended up angry, resentful, and confused. It took me some years to learn that my core desires are not rooted in substantive service but in reflection and care for people's spiritual and emotional well-being.

I need a balance between times of solitude and social get-togethers. Too much time with people frazzles me—I need time to think, read, slow down, be outdoors—yet I also need a little casual time each week just to hang out with friends. I need a larger chunk of time for a full-day or half-day retreat at least every six months, either by myself or with a small group of people who enjoy silence and reflection without a lot of hoopla or organized activity. It's also important for me to intentionally include some moments of play in my daily routine, or life begins to lose its luster.

As I walk my dog, Molly, she demonstrates to me one way to "stay tuned" to God. "Heel," I say to her, and she falls in with the rhythm of my stride—until she's distracted by the loud roar of a passing truck or a barking dog along our path. "Heel, Molly," I remind her. She glances at me, at the distraction, back to me, and then falls in line again. "Good girl," I say, as she once again tunes in to my voice and the pace we're keeping together. For me, time I spend in nature thinking, reading, and reflecting weaves natural reminders of God's presence into my days. I can also count on Molly to interrupt me regularly for a light-hearted round of catch with her stuffed "froggie."

When Frank and I moved to McKinney, we noticed that a robin had nested on a low branch beside our driveway. As three hatchlings gradually pecked their way out of their baby blue shells, we watched from behind binoculars at an upstairs window, feeling as if Mrs. Robin were personally welcoming us to the neighborhood. She'd shared the joy of birth with us. The babies grew fast. Within days their fuzzy down had turned to feathers, and it seemed Mrs. Robin was bringing a fresh supply of earthworms and bugs each time I peered through the binoculars.

Then we noticed there were only two baby birds. Perhaps one had been pushed from the nest or for some reason did not thrive. Within days the two remaining nestlings appeared to be outgrowing their home, and we knew they'd be flying away soon. One day as I was coming home from work, I decided to take an up-close peek into the nest as I pulled into the driveway. I must have shocked the little birds, now nearly as large as their mama, and they fluttered out of the nest to a low place in the grass nearby.

Oh no! I silently gasped. *They're out of the nest, and it's too soon. Please God, help them! They can't get back in.* As I watched the scared little birds walking around on the driveway, Mrs. Robin appeared with a mouthful of bugs. But the babies were afraid in their new surroundings, even with their mama nearby. They'd left home before it was time. Mrs. Robin chirped and fluttered back to the nest as if to say, "Come on up. This is how to do it. Flap hard! You can make it!" But as the babies fluttered their wings, they could get only about three feet above the ground.

I had wanted only to peek at the baby birds, but now I had invaded their little lives, perhaps even brought on imminent premature death. Rushing into the house I grabbed an old sheet to throw over the babies in hopes of catching them and returning them to their nest. But after spending more than an hour in failed attempts, I settled into a porch chair, a depressed, helpless intruder. The moral? There is a season, a natural flow, to everything in nature, and I had messed with it. Rushing God's timing has its consequences, and I could only hope that God would somehow intervene and make up for my intrusion on his natural way of doing things. I didn't like the lesson of the day, as is sometimes true for all of us as we live in God's presence, but I would remember it well. And I would continue to see reminders of God's caring ways as I observed nature.

For me, it's easy to sense God's presence as I watch animals, birds, trees, and other living things. His ways of relating to people are clearly observable as well—it's all there, the good and the bad, the right and the wrong ways of doing things. What are the "techniques in the search for grace" that fit *for you?* At this time in your life what do you need more of and less of? Can you name one thing that must be a part of your routine if you are going to be able to stay aware of God's presence throughout your days? Are you a natural substantive servant who finds fulfillment and senses God's presence as you do good deeds and meet practical needs for others? Do you need time to think, reflect, discuss your spiritual life with a close friend, or write about it? Do you relish a quiet day of spiritual retreat several times a year, or does that seem like a waste of time to you?

Nobody is wrong or right; we're just all different. We don't get to pick out our temperaments and spiritual gifts as if we're ordering a life out of a catalog. Instead, we come to an understanding and acceptance of the life God has ordered uniquely for us. We begin cherishing the lives he has given us as gifts, celebrating our relationship with him, practicing his presence, walking with him to an unforced rhythm, and trusting that in a way only God understands, our lives will bear fruit.

It's helpful to gain some understanding of what we need to weave into our lives so that we can thrive and feel safe and comfortable in the lap of our King. There, as our thoughts, deeds, and feelings find their resting place, we may also sometimes experience those "delightful and delicious feelings" Brother Lawrence talked about as he drew near to God's holy presence.

THE CALL OF THE DISTANT PIPER

• • •

I AM THE VOICE OF ONE CALLING

IN THE DESERT.

John 1:23

We see a playful glimpse of truth about the winsome nature of an encounter with a holy presence and the longing it creates for something more, in Kenneth Grahame's tale *The Wind in the Willows*. At one point in the story, woodland friends Rat and Mole go searching for Mr. Otter's little son, who has been lost for several days. As they climb into Rat's boat and go gliding through the reeds and rushes on their mission of charity, the sound of distant piping beckons them. Rat sits up and listens intently.

" 'It's gone!' sighed the Rat, sinking back in his seat again. 'So beautiful and strange and new! Since it was to end so soon, I almost wish I had never heard it. For it has roused a longing in me that is pain, and nothing seems worthwhile but just to hear that sound once more and go on listening to it forever. No! There it is again!' he cried, alert once more. Entranced, he was silent for a long space, spellbound."[8]

At first Mole hears nothing and looks at Rat curiously, merely keeping the boat moving. But eventually he becomes aware of the wondrous piping that is holding Rat's attention and is himself transfixed. After a time they move further up the stream, where they moor the boat and step out onto an island.

" 'This is the place of my song-dream, the place the music played to me,' whispered the Rat, as if in a trance."[9]

He had been through these waters before, heard the happy call of the distant piping, and encountered a mysterious presence.

"Then suddenly the Mole felt a great awe fall upon him, an awe that turned his muscles to water, bowed his head, and rooted his feet to the ground. It was no panic terror—indeed he felt wonderfully at peace and happy—but it was an awe that smote and held him and, without seeing, he knew it could only mean that some august Presence was very, very near."[10]

Led by the call of the distant piping and drawing closer to the mysterious presence, the two little animals were guided to the place where the lost baby otter lay—still alive.

"Then the two animals, crouching to the earth, bowed their heads and did worship."[11]

We can be overcome by a sense of awe and wonder as we become aware of God's holy presence hovering near. One winter day I was peeling potatoes at the kitchen sink, preoccupied by anxious thoughts of a beloved family member who had just entered a drug-rehabilitation program. I shot up a spontaneous prayer: *God, don't forget about him. Guide him through these dark troubled waters, won't you? He's drifted so far out to sea, and we can't see him, can't reach him. He can't hear us, so please call him back.*

Suddenly a loud clattering of birds caught my attention and interrupted the sound of the largo section of a classical concerto playing in the background. I looked out the kitchen window to see a flock of blackbirds lowering themselves into the clearing in back of the house. For a few moments the birds picked around in the dead grass, gathering a winter day's feeding. Then, as if choreographed to fit with the transition into the upbeat allegro part in the concerto, the birds' wings began to flutter. The flock rose in unison a few feet into the air, then changed directions and flew off like a handful of shimmering black glitter flung across a cold, gray sky.

As the two-minute blackbird ballet ended, my worried mind was awestruck with a mysterious reminder that a holy presence hovered—not only over me but also over my loved one. As surely as God had orchestrated the birds' feeding, the timing of his visit to my troubled soul, and the reminder of his presence through the flock of birds, he was just as surely in charge of all creation, and I could rest in that knowledge. God would hold things up, and I didn't have to understand just how all of it would work. I could get on with the dinner preparations with a little lighter heart and lingering peace as I savored the call of the divine Presence.

One day we will fully experience moment-to-moment intimacy with our Lord. Won't it be wonderful? Our days of gathering techniques to help us find ways to live "in grace" will come to an end as we see the Personification of all we've only faintly glimpsed in this life. We will have our day of sitting comfortably in the lap of our King.

In the Meantime, we find our fitting way of serving him, peel our potatoes, and long for what is to come.

• • •

LET US GO RIGHT INTO THE

PRESENCE OF GOD, WITH TRUE

HEARTS FULLY TRUSTING HIM.

Hebrews 10:22, NLT

LIVING IN GOD'S FAIRY TALE

Letting His Love Write Today's Chapter

• • •

JUST AS I SHOULD SEEK IN A DESERT

FOR CLEAN WATER, OR TOIL AT THE NORTH POLE

TO MAKE A COMFORTABLE FIRE, SO I SHALL

SEARCH THE LAND OF VOID AND VISION

UNTIL I FIND SOMETHING FRESH LIKE WATER,

AND COMFORTING LIKE FIRE; UNTIL I FIND

SOME PLACE IN ETERNITY WHERE

I AM LITERALLY AT HOME.

G. K. Chesterton[1]

When we begin our lives with Christ, it's as if we've stepped into our own handwritten storybook with him. It starts with Once upon a Time, and with our bright future before us, full of hopes, dreams, and longings for ourselves and the people we love, we think we've arrived at Happily Ever After. We learn about Christ's character and his ways and begin the gradual process of taking on his likeness. At some point, reality starts to set in. Disappointments come. Perhaps we fail at something we thought we could succeed in. Relationships change. Even when we're trusting God, doing our best, and talking things over with him as we go along, somehow our dreams don't unfold in the way we hoped they would.

Life seldom turns out as we plan it or hope it will. Still, in the midst of its ups and downs, we begin to see that even though the idealized dreams we once had are not coming true, hidden blessings beyond what we ever could have dreamed are waiting for us to uncover day by day, through life as it really is—not as we thought it should be.

Jesus said to his disciples, "Love each other. Just as I have loved you, you should love each other" (John 13:34, NLT). It sounds easy, doesn't it? But you have probably found, as I have, that loving and being loved does not always turn out to be what we expected. Sometimes other people try to give us love, and we don't recognize it because it doesn't come packaged the way we hoped it would. Or maybe we try to demonstrate love to someone dear to us, but they don't seem to "get it." Giving and receiving love in the midst of life's anxieties, fears, rejections, successes, failures, joys, and sorrows presents its challenges.

As I was unpacking boxes after Frank and I moved to McKinney, I came across a Ginny doll I'd given to my mother as a gift for her eighty-third birthday—her last. When my sister, Jan, and I went to California for Mother's funeral, each of us collected some childhood treasures Mother had put away for us in an old trunk—the Elsie cups we drank hot chocolate from each Christmas Eve while we were growing up, the clay ducks and toothpick holders we molded in third-grade art class, baby shoes, pictures, reminders of the past.

As Jan and I shared our memories of the stowed treasures and prepared the items for shipping to our homes, my stepdad walked over with the Ginny doll. "Do you remember this?" Ray asked, holding her out to me.

"Oh, that's Mother's birthday gift from last year," I said. With a deep desire to connect with Mother as I'd been able to do only a few times, I had puzzled over what gift might speak love to her in a way she could get the message, even with a decreased mental capacity during the beginning stages of Alzheimer's. *Perhaps a new gown, since she seldom dresses or gets out of the house. No, that's so ordinary. Maybe a new purse. Except what use would she have for it?*

Then one day as I was shopping, I passed a small shop that carried classic dolls, antique and new—Sweet Sues, Terry Lees, even a few Tiny Tears and Bonnie Braids. When I spied a brown-haired Ginny doll in the window, my heart leapt as I remembered the Christmas Mother and Dad gave Ginnys to my sister and me. *Would Mother enjoy this doll?* I wondered. She had given many dolls to me through the years, but she spoke of only one rag doll she'd owned as a child. *Yes,* I decided.

The store clerk boxed Ginny up and stuck in a tiny comb and brush set that came with her as I briefly explained the doll's destiny. "I hope she brings a lot of joy to your Mother in her old age." I hoped so too. With three states between us, I mailed the gift from Texas to California and didn't get to see Mother's response when she opened it.

"She looks different from what I remember," I told Ray as he handed the doll to me.

"Yes," Ray said. "Every morning your mother would sit here in the front room, look out the window as people walked by after breakfast, and hold the doll and brush her hair."

"That's the difference," I said, remembering that when I bought her she had tight ringlet curls. "Now she has a frizzy do."

"Yes. Your mother loved that doll, held it, and played with it. Now that she's passed on, she'd want you to have it back."

That was five years ago. Today as I unpacked a few treasured belongings, my heart warmed as I placed Mother's well-loved Ginny on top of a display case. To me, the doll stood as a symbol that even though Mother and I never understood each other very well and the two of us had not shared much closeness, we'd finally found a way to share love. When I'd discovered the lavish love of God for me during my mid-forties, it released something inside me that I'd involuntarily held back from my mother. The blessing I had always hoped she would give me as her daughter—of being seen, heard, and known for who I was—was something I already had because God had given it to me. Then I could, in turn, pass love on to my mother with no expectations for what I might get back. The doll's frizzy hairdo proved to me that Mother had gotten the message, felt my love, and embraced it as she played with the doll.

Later that evening after Frank and I had finished our unpacking for the day, Scott and his new wife, Jane, came for a small family get-together in honor of Jane's thirtieth birthday. Life must go on, even in the midst of moving. Frank had created a wonderful aroma in the backyard as he prepared to grill steaks over pecan wood. Brent, who loves to cook, arrived with a loaf of bread and an apple tart he had baked earlier that day, along with makings for a summer squash stir-fry and garlic mashed potatoes. As they all came into the kitchen, my sister, Jan, and I were talking on the phone. We passed the cordless around, reminisced about our last visit at her home in northern California, and set a tentative date for our next one.

Brent got out a cutting board and started chopping vegetables for his stir-fry, and Scott went upstairs and began hooking up a new computer monitor he'd brought over for my office, since he'd recently bought a new one for himself. He had begun the process of upgrading my system with some of his slightly used discards. With all the men busy, I got to sit on the front porch with Jane until the Texas mosquitoes drove us back inside.

After a gourmet birthday dinner Jane opened her gifts, and Brent tossed his meatless T-bone out in the backyard for Molly to gnaw on, which she did—with gusto. We settled into chairs in our living room to relax a few minutes before they all had to be on their way. It was quite an ordinary evening, and yet as we all hugged and my two sons and new daughter-in-law left, I knew something indescribable and wonderful had happened.

It occurred to me that I was surrounded by love and blessings. Though they had not always come to me in ways I once anticipated at the beginning of my Christian life, I was learning to recognize some of love's hidden forms. Three of our four children had come for dinner with Frank and me (I have two sons, a stepson, and a daughter-in-law), and in very simple, ordinary ways we had shared love.

After they had left, Frank and I sat back down. Frank picked up a book to read, and my thoughts settled on gratitude for my children and some of the other people I care about. Molly sprawled at my feet, content as she could be. As her round, golden eyes stared lovingly into mine, my mind flashed back to the day Brent drove me to East Texas to pick Molly out. She had come from a large litter of eight-week-old chocolate labs, and Brent gave her to me as a belated Christmas gift, accompanied by a copy of *Water Dog,* a developmental training guide for labs.

Though I had owned dogs before, none of them had ever taken over my heart as Molly had. I wasn't quite sure just how it happened. But I thought perhaps it had something to do with what it meant to Brent to give her to me—the care he'd taken in choosing her from the litter as he snapped his fingers to test her hearing and tossed a stick to check her instincts. I knew he'd saved up his money to buy her at a time when he didn't have much spare cash. Most important, he had bought me a dog like his very own favorite.

Brent's chocolate lab, Boomer, had become the apple of his eye as they hunted, hiked, and hung out together for more than five years. Watching the two of them become such good friends had turned us into a lab family as Scott soon adopted Gretzky, and Molly had added a dimension of fun and playfulness to Frank's and my lives. Tonight as Molly lay beside my living-room chair, I gave her an affectionate scratch behind the ear. "Hey, girlfriend," I said, as her tail started beating rhythmically against the carpet.

Next my mind wandered to a time when Scott had vowed he would never marry. Hurt by our family breakup when he was fourteen, he didn't want to take any more risks. I recalled several times over the years when the two of us had gotten together at Papasito's to talk something over or just catch up on each other's lives. Once I told him how much I had missed his company during his last two years of high school, when he went to live with his dad and Brent stayed with me. He told me he had missed me, too, but especially he'd missed Brent.

The divorce had not only split the parents but had also torn brother from brother. We'd talked about Scott's lingering feelings of guilt after he went to live with his dad. He had thought that if he hadn't been so strong willed, things might have been different, the divorce wouldn't have happened, all of us could have been together—typical feelings for children in the aftermath of divorce. I had repeatedly reassured him over the years that nothing about the divorce was his fault, but the message didn't seem to sink in. We had discussed his reluctance to date, to trust, to risk being hurt again. Then we had hugged and gone to our separate homes. The particular evening I was recalling was one of those times when Scott and I had deeply connected, and I think our relationship was a little closer from that point on. A few years later he had found Jane, and now they were married.

Another "Papasito's memory" floated into my mind, this one of a recent meeting, the week before Scott's wedding. I wanted to have a mother-son heart-to-heart, knowing things would be different after his marriage, as they should be. In preparation I had typed out the words to "Cole's Song" from the movie *Mr. Holland's Opus*. To me, the song put words to a parent's (perhaps overdue) acknowledgment of an adult child's unique individuality and beauty, whether or not it came in ways the parent had planned.

I was trying to communicate something to Scott, and I didn't quite know how to do it. So I did what I sometimes do in those cases and talked through the theme of a movie. Scott hadn't seen *Mr. Holland's Opus,* so I reviewed the highlights of the story line something like this:

Glenn Holland takes a job as a music teacher at Kennedy High to put food on the table for his wife and baby boy while he prepares for his "life-defining work" writing symphonies. The ideal life Mr. Holland envisions for his family takes a turn down the road to disillusionment when they learn that their toddler son, Cole, is deaf. Mr. Holland, a musician whose head is filled with uncomposed symphonies and plans to raise a family of musicians, has a deaf son—the ultimate letdown for a musician. As time passes, the job Mr. Holland thought would be a temporary fill-in position ends up lasting over thirty years.

In the meantime, Cole grows up, learns sign language, excels in school, and gets a job teaching deaf students. Mr. Holland and Cole don't share the common interests, goals, and plans Mr. Holland dreamed of at the time of Cole's birth. The distractions of busyness, financial needs, and Mr. Holland's preoccupation with composing music take up his time, further lessening any chances of a closer relationship between himself and his son.

Over time Mr. Holland's drivenness gradually mellows him into a gifted teacher who turns kids on to music. As his vision of writing famous symphonies slowly slips out of his hands, it takes some time for him to get past the anger and hurt over his lost dream. But then a new vision begins to evolve—the vision of living life in acceptance and gratitude for life as it is and not as he once thought it should be. Mr. Holland also begins to glimpse fulfillment in ways he had not been able to envision earlier.

Finally, in a moment that touches the bottom of any parent's heart, Mr. Holland pauses in the middle of an orchestral performance he's conducting to sing *and sign* the words to a song he has written for his deaf son—"Cole's Song"—in a language he can understand. Tears fill Cole's eyes as they lock with his dad's in a gaze of mutual compassion and love. The recognition and validation Cole had always been trying to get from his dad, the seeing and being seen, the hearing and being heard, the knowing and being known—all passed between the two of them in that climactic moment.

This was not how Mr. Holland had once pictured the fulfillment of his youthful dream of becoming a symphony composer. Yet in that moment as he found himself surrounded by friends and people who loved and accepted him, he realized that he had accomplished a very important goal—learning how to love and be loved.

As I finished recounting the movie's theme to Scott that evening at Papasito's, I told him I felt my Christian life had been a bit like Mr. Holland's life. I set out to be an ideal Christian wife and mother, teaching Bible stories and memorizing proverbs with him and his brother as they grew up, serving in the church, trying to have strong faith and raise a Christian family so we could have good lives. But in my youthful dreams I knew nothing of the heart of God or how to teach my kids about his real character—his goodness and love for us no matter what happens—since I didn't even know these things for myself. Disappointments came. Plans got changed. We all had to find new dreams. I didn't know how to talk about these things to my sons as they were growing up.

Scott listened as I explained that being blessed as a Christian was not at all like I once thought or planned or dreamed. I said that I had discovered God's grace unexpectedly through my failures instead of through my strengths; affection of other people through vulnerability instead of through perfection; gratitude for a difficult relationship with my mother through recognizing our similarities rather than our differences; the love of my adult children through their acceptance of me as I am, rather than because I was the ideal example I had once planned to be. I explained that for me, being blessed was about giving and receiving love.

We talked about how in our family we had done a lot of growing up together over the years. Scott and Brent learned some things from their dad and me and from their stepparents and others, and I learned a lot from my sons, too. Watching Scott's life evolve created a picture for me of one way that trust can break down, what it takes to rebuild it, and the wounds we're left with. Brent had always been a tenderhearted, nature-loving type of guy who at age ten once brought home a wounded blackbird in a paper sack when a buddy's father took him on his first hunting trip. Brent had fired a random shot into the air, not thinking about how it would feel to actually shoot a bird. The bird had died in two days despite a regular supply of water and worms. Brent grew to enjoy the outdoor sports of hunting and fishing yet always with respect for wildlife, never killing what he would not be using as food. That tenderness of heart was still there, though it emerged in different forms. From watching his life, I've learned that it can be difficult for men to remain tender-hearted and still thrive in this world. I hoped he would do both.

I didn't understand what brought these recollections to mind that evening after Jane's birthday party. Maybe the gratitude in my heart for a new daughter-in-law, for simple ways to exchange love with the people I care about. My life had turned out so vastly different from the vision I once had for my family. And yet Mother's Ginny doll stood on the display case as a fresh reminder that God's grace reaches down through generations of flawed, frail human love, not wiping out our problems, pain, and disappointments but loving us through—and beyond—our limitations.

> Our lives may have turned out so vastly different from the vision we once had, and yet fresh reminders of God's grace reach down through generations of flawed, frail human love, not wiping out our problems, pain, and disappointments but loving us through—and beyond—our limitations.

• • •

THIS IS THE KIND OF LOVE WE ARE TALKING ABOUT—NOT THAT WE ONCE UPON A TIME LOVED GOD, BUT THAT HE LOVED US AND SENT HIS SON AS A SACRIFICE TO CLEAR AWAY OUR SINS AND THE DAMAGE THEY'VE DONE TO OUR RELATIONSHIP WITH GOD.

1 John 4:10, *THE MESSAGE*

Finding Today's Treasure

• • •

The kingdom of heaven is like
treasure hidden in a field. When a man
found it, he hid it again, and then
in his joy went and sold all he
had and bought that field.

Matthew 13:44

Have you become disillusioned with your life, your relationships with family and friends? Have your plans and dreams changed drastically from the vision you once had for your Christian life? Perhaps if you had known up front that it was to be a life of blessing you didn't want, writing an opus you didn't want to compose, with people you would inevitably hurt as you tried to love them, you might not have had the nerve to place your faith in Christ as your Savior at all. It sounded so wonderful in the beginning, didn't it: trust Christ as your Savior and Lord; he'll give you an abundant life of blessing and an eternal home in glory.

And yet it *is* true. It's true not only for Happily Ever After but for here and now—in the Meantime. We do have today. To live, to love, to trust Christ beyond our failures and disappointments. To discover hidden blessings and unexpected ways we are loved, unplanned dreams beyond our expectations—treasures waiting to be discovered as we search for them like children peeking under rocks, finding the ones that sparkle brightest at the bottom of a mud puddle.

At a national counselors conference, Dr. Keith Miller spoke to a large audience about his concern that the body of Christ has a lot to learn about loving—especially about loving others through our confusion, disappointments, and failure. He told how his public ministry and success as an author and lecturer came to a sudden halt and ended his marriage after he became involved in an affair. "I'd succeeded at almost everything I tried, and I didn't know how to fail," he said.[2]

He explained how he had turned to his Christian friends and his church because he knew he had done wrong and needed their help, direction, and support. But he was shocked to discover that the church didn't know how to help him. Now, twenty years later, he had written a book, *The Secret Life of the Soul*,[3] and had returned to the lecture circuit to help Christian leaders and counselors learn practical skills for loving and being loved through successes and failures, good times and bad.

"Who was the first person outside your family who made you feel loved?" Dr. Miller asked, explaining that family members didn't count because those relationships are often loaded with guilt or manipulation or control issues. "Not what that person *did,* just who the person was and what he or she looked like." Dr. Miller clarified his direction as men and women turned to the person next to them and began to share ways they'd felt loved as a child. Instantly my third grade teacher, Miss Shanks, came to mind. She was a kind, warm-spirited woman with a short, ample body. Her Buster Brown—cut salt-and-pepper hair framed a face that loved kids, and we all knew it whether she sported smiles or frowns. While I was still sharing my thoughts with the woman beside me, Dr. Miller interrupted us.

"Okay, now share what the person *did* to make you feel loved." I recalled hearing Miss Shanks tell me that I was a good speller and could be a winner in the upcoming spelling contest. With confidence I would not have had without her caring encouragement, I tied for first place with two other girls. The colleague beside me had also recalled an elementary school teacher who first made her feel loved by pushing her on a swing. As we shared our thoughts, Dr. Miller interrupted us again, soliciting a sampling of our collective response to share with the entire audience. People called out their comments as a volunteer secretary jotted them down on an overhead:

"My neighbor taught me how to make cookies."

"My Sunday school teacher turned up the heat in the classroom because I was cold."

"My teacher told me I could be a winner."

"My teacher pushed me on a swing."

After recording ten or twelve responses, Dr. Miller then summarized his point: it's often the little, everyday things we do that make others feel loved, and since God *is* love, all acts of love and kindness actually have their source in him. Then Dr. Miller went through our list of combined responses once again, this time replacing the person's name or title with the word *Jesus.*

Jesus taught me how to make cookies.

Jesus turned up the heat in the classroom because I was cold.

Jesus told me I could be a winner.

Jesus pushed me on a swing.

The flow of intimate love through imperfect human beings takes on a likeness to Christ's love manifested on the cross: *"Just as I have loved you,* you should love each other" (John 13:34, NLT, italics added). All good gifts ultimately come from God, through Christ, to us as receivers. As contributors and givers, whatever we do or say or give or know or believe, it all counts as *nothing* if it doesn't come from a heart filled with love—not because the person we're demonstrating love to is so lovable but because we who know God's love for us are passing it on to others in his name.

Although the dreams we once had have become tattered and torn, knowing each other, accepting each other, and giving and receiving flawed human love mixed with God's love make it all worthwhile. Even if someone you care about rejects your love, perhaps in a broken family relationship, you can still send your love through the circuitry of prayer and cherish that person in your heart even if you cannot directly express your affection person-to-person.

The Beatitudes take on deeper meaning as we come to understand the idea of "blessing" in ways we may not have previously considered: "You're blessed when you're at the end of your rope. With less of you there is more of God and his rule. You're blessed when you feel you've lost what is most dear to you. Only then can you be embraced by the One most dear to you. You're blessed when you're content with just who you are—no more, no less. That's the moment you find yourselves proud owners of everything that can't be bought" (Matthew 5:3-5, *THE MESSAGE*).

As Christians, we may have expected an instant transformation into Happily Ever After the moment we came to know Christ. But God does not magically sprinkle glimmering beams of fairy dust over us. Instead, through disguised blessings, unexpected turns in the road, our changing lives encounter Jesus Christ—who *never* changes. This is what makes the gospel like a fairy tale—it asks you to look beyond what is visible and see absolute truth.

Christ calls us still to come "just as I am," moment by moment. Can you hear him? He walks with us now, creating an incurable faith, a longing in our hearts for something beyond this life. Can you sense his presence? Your tale—the true story of your life as it really is and not as you wish it were or thought it should be—is the journey God has promised to make with you, to love you through, during all these days of the Meantime.

• • •

I HAVE LOVED YOU WITH AN EVERLASTING
LOVE; I HAVE DRAWN YOU WITH
LOVING-KINDNESS. I WILL BUILD YOU
UP AGAIN AND YOU WILL BE REBUILT. . . . THERE
WILL BE A DAY WHEN WATCHMEN CRY
OUT ON THE HILLS OF EPHRAIM, "COME,
LET US GO UP TO ZION,
TO THE LORD OUR GOD."

Jeremiah 31:3, 6

notes

CHAPTER 1

1. Frederick Buechner, *Telling the Truth: The Gospel As Tragedy, Comedy and Fairy Tale* (San Francisco: HarperSanFrancisco, 1977), 98.
2. Bruno Bettelheim, *The Uses of Enchantment: The Meaning and Importance of Fairy Tales* (New York: Vintage Books, A Division of Random House, 1989), 10.
3. Dallas Willard, *The Divine Conspiracy: Rediscovering Our Hidden Life in God* (San Francisco: HarperCollins Publishers, 1998), 76.
4. Buechner, *Telling the Truth*, 98.
5. Brennan Manning, *The Ragamuffin Gospel* (Sisters, Oreg.: Multnomah Books, 1990), 112.
6. A. W. Tozer, *The Pursuit of God* (Harrisburg, Pa.: Christian Publications, 1943), 33.
7. Oswald Chambers, quoted in David McCasland, *Oswald Chambers: Abandoned to God* (Nashville: Discovery House Books, 1993), 74.
8. Larry Crabb, *Connecting* (Dallas: Word Publishing, 1997), audiotape.
9. John Eldredge, *The Journey of Desire* (Nashville: Thomas Nelson, 2000), 86.
10. Helen Keller, quoted in Carolyn Costin, *Monte Nido Newsletter*, August 1998, Malibu, California.

CHAPTER 2

1. A. W. Tozer, *The Pursuit of God* (Harrisburg, Pa.: Christian Publications, 1943), 34.
2. *The NIV Study Bible*, New International Version (Grand Rapids: Zondervan Publishing House, 1995), from note on John 12:32.
3. G. K. Chesterton, *Orthodoxy* (San Francisco: Ignatius Press, 1995), 55.
4. Thomas Keating, *Invitation to Love* (New York: Continuum Publishing, 2001), 44.
5. David Hazard, *Early Will I Seek You: A 40-Day Journey in the Company of Augustine* (Minneapolis: Bethany House Publishers, 1973), 59.
6. Roy and Revel Hession, *We Would See Jesus* (Fort Washington, Pa.: Christian Literature Crusade, 1984), 5.

CHAPTER 3

1. Oswald Chambers, quoted in Diane Langberg, *Lessons Learned in the Therapist's Chair*, a featured audiotaped presentation of the American Association of Christian Counselors, 1996.
2. G. K. Chesterton, quoted by Iris Pearce in a lecture given at St. Francis Episcopal Church in Dallas, Texas, 2000.
3. Henri Nouwen, *Life of the Beloved* (New York: Crossroad Publishing, 1997), 26.
4. Brennan Manning, *Come Now, My Love* (Minneapolis: Growing in Grace Media Ministries, 1995), audiotape.
5. A. W. Tozer, *The Pursuit of God* (Harrisburg, Pa.: Christian Publications, 1943), 31.
6. Paraphrased from Psalm 139:23-24
7. Richard Alves, quoted in Billy Grammer, *Perspectives on Pursuing Bold Love* (Dallas: Fellowship Bible Church Dallas Counseling Center, 1997), audiotape series.
8. Paul Tillich, *The Courage to Be* (New Haven, Conn.: Yale University Press, 2000), 74.
9. Richard Rohr, *Simplicity* (New York: Crossroad Publishing, 1998), 58.
10. Augustine, quoted in Kathleen Norris, *Amazing Grace* (New York: Riverhead Books, 1998), 368.

CHAPTER 4

1. C. S. Lewis, quoted in Leanne Payne, *Real Presence: The Glory of Christ with Us and within Us* (Grand Rapids: Baker Books, 1995), 45.
2. Iris Pearce, from a lecture given at St. Francis Episcopal Church in Dallas, Texas, 2001.
3. Archibald Hart, "Has Self-Esteem Lost Its Way?" *Christian Counseling Today* 9, no. 1 (2001).
4. John Eldredge, *The Journey of Desire* (Nashville: Thomas Nelson, 2000), 81.
5. Henri Nouwen, "Living As the Beloved," audiotape of a public address given at the Church of the Resurrection, Dallas, Texas, 1993.
6. Brennan Manning, *A Stranger to Self-Hatred* (Denville, N.J.: Dimension Books, 1982), 29.
7. G. K. Chesterton, *Orthodoxy* (San Francisco: Ignatius Press, 1995), 54–55.
8. Manning, *Stranger to Self-Hatred*, 28.
9. Teresa of Avila, quoted in Billy Grammer, *Perspectives on Pursuing Bold Love* (Dallas: Fellowship Bible Church Dallas Counseling Center, 1997), audiotape series.
10. Emily Dickinson, No. 318 in *The Complete Poems of Emily Dickinson*, ed. Thomas H. Johnson (Boston: Little, Brown, 1960).
11. Frederick Buechner, *Telling the Truth: The Gospel As Tragedy, Comedy and Fairy Tale* (San Francisco: HarperSanFrancisco, 1977), 80.

CHAPTER 5

1. Dallas Willard, *The Divine Conspiracy: Rediscovering Our Hidden Life in God* (San Francisco: HarperCollins Publishers, 1998), 76.

2. Richard Foster, quoted in Sheila Walsh, *Honestly* (Grand Rapids: Zondervan, 1996), 117.

3. Unpublished writing by Kathy Doerge © 2002. Used by permission.

4. J. Keith Miller, *The Secret Life of the Soul* (Nashville: Broadman and Holman Publishers, 1997), 15.

5. Sheila Walsh, *Honestly* (Grand Rapids: Zondervan, 1996), 47.

6. Ibid., 57.

7. Brennan Manning, *The Ragamuffin Gospel* (Sisters, Oreg.: Multnomah, 1990), 21.

8. Paul Tournier, *A Place for You* (New York: Harper and Row, 1968), 163.

CHAPTER 6

1. Henri Nouwen, *The Inner Voice of Love* (New York: Doubleday, 1996), 84.

2. Robertson McQuilkin, *A Promise Kept* (Wheaton, Ill.: Tyndale House Publishers, 1998), 49.

3. Ibid., 52.

4. Jeanne Guyon, *Experiencing the Depths of Jesus Christ*, Library of Spiritual Classics, vol. 2, 3rd ed. (Auburn, Maine: Christian Books Publishing, 1999), 46.

5. Monty Roberts, *The Man Who Listens to Horses*, quoted by Carolyn Costin at Twelfth Annual Symposium of International Association of Eating Disorders Professionals, Orlando, Florida, 1998.

6. Steve Brown, "The Law: God's Gateway to Freedom," *Key Life* magazine, summer 2002.

7. Henri Nouwen, *Finding My Way Home* (New York: Crossroad Publishing, 2001), 114.

8. E. Stanley Jones, *Victory through Surrender* (Nashville: Abingdon Press, 1980), 54.

9. Ann and Barry Ulanov, *Primary Speech: A Psychology of Prayer* (Atlanta: John Knox Press, 1982), 20.

10. Nouwen, *Inner Voice of Love*, 9–10.

11. Bill Zimmerman, *The Little Book of Joy* (Center City, Minn.: Hazelden, 1995).

12. Nouwen, *Finding My Way Home*, 112.

CHAPTER 7

1. Jeanne Guyon, *Experiencing the Depths of Jesus Christ*, Library of Spiritual Classics, vol. 2, 3rd ed. (Auburn, Maine: Christian Books Publishing, 1999), 141.

2. William James, quoted in Anne Morrow Lindbergh, *Gift from the Sea* (New York: Pantheon Books, 1955), 50.

3. Richard Rohr, *Simplicity: The Art of Living* (New York: Crossroad Publishing, 1998), 51.

4. Ed McNulty, "Celebration of Dance in Cinema," *Christianity and the Arts* (2000): 21.

5. Frederick Buechner, *The Longing for Home* (San Francisco: HarperSanFrancisco, 1996), 17.

6. Julie Kelly and Rosalie Devonshire, *Taking Charge of Fibromyalgia* (Wayzata, Minn.: Fibromyalgia Educational Systems, 1991), 16.

7. Archibald Hart, *The Hidden Link Between Adrenaline and Stress* (Dallas: Word Publishing, 1995), 27.

8. Christiane Northrup, *Women's Bodies, Women's Wisdom* (New York: Bantam Books, 1998), 34–35.

9. Dallas Willard, *The Divine Conspiracy: Rediscovering Our Hidden Life in God* (San Francisco: HarperCollins Publishers, 1998), 133.

10. Percy Bysshe Shelley, "To a Skylark," *One Hundred and One Famous Poems* (Chicago: Contemporary Books, 1958), 25.

Chapter 8

1. David Roper, *Psalm 23: The Song of a Passionate Heart* (Grand Rapids: Discovery House Publishers, 1994), 66.

2. Brennan Manning, *The Ragamuffin Gospel* (Sisters, Oreg.: Multnomah, 1990), 168.

3. George Macdonald, quoted in David Roper, *Psalm 23*, 74.

4. Roy and Revel Hession, *We Would See Jesus* (Fort Washington, Pa.: Christian Literature Crusade, 1984), 26.

5. Julian of Norwich, *The Revelation of Divine Love*, trans. Edmund Colledge and James Walsh (New York: Paulist Press, 1978), 193–94.

6. A. W. Tozer, *The Pursuit of God* (Harrisburg, Pa.: Christian Publications, 1943), 38.

7. Meister Eckhart, quoted in O. B. Duane, *The Origins of Wisdom: Mysticism* (London: Brockhampton Press, 1997), 72.

8. Frederick Buechner, *The Magnificent Defeat* (New York: Seabury Press, 1966), 48.

9. Ann and Barry Ulanov, *Primary Speech: A Psychology of Prayer* (Atlanta: John Knox Press, 1982), 23.

Chapter 9

1. Dallas Willard, *The Divine Conspiracy: Rediscovering Our Hidden Life in God* (San Francisco: HarperCollins Publishers, 1998), 49.

2. Henri Nouwen, *Here and Now* (New York: Crossroad Publishing, 1994), 90.

3. Ann and Barry Ulanov, *Primary Speech: A Psychology of Prayer* (Atlanta: John Knox Press, 1982), 15.

4. C. S. Lewis, *The Lion, the Witch, and the Wardrobe* (New York: Collier Books, 1970), 23–26.

5. Teresa of Avila, *The Interior Castle*, trans. and ed. E. Allison Peers (New York: Doubleday, 1961), 28, 31.

6. Willard, *Divine Conspiracy*, 40.

7. Garry Landreth, *Play Therapy: The Art of the Relationship* (Bristol, Pa.: Accelerated Development, 1991), 3.

8. Paul Tillich, *The Shaking of the Foundations* (New York: Scribner's, 1948), 161–62.

9. A. W. Tozer, quoted in David Roper, *Psalm 23: The Song of a Passionate Heart* (Grand Rapids: Discovery House Publishers, 1994), 57.

10. Henri Nouwen, quoted in David Roper, *Psalm 23*, 58.

11. Jill Briscoe, "Rest Stops," an address given at a Breakaway conference.

12. Anthony Bloom, *Beginning to Pray* (New York: Paulist Press, 1970), 112–13.
13. Thomas à Kempis, quoted in David Roper, *Psalm 23*, 59.
14. David Roper, *Psalm 23*, 54.

CHAPTER 10

1. Frederick Buechner, *The Hungering Dark* (New York: Harper and Row, 1969), 106–7.
2. John of the Cross, *Dark Night of the Soul*, trans. and ed. E. Allison Peers (New York: Doubleday, 1990), 100.
3. Dionysius, quoted in O. B. Duane, *The Origins of Wisdom: Mysticism* (London: Brockhampton Press, 1997), 52.
4. Frederick Buechner, *Listening to Your Life* (San Francisco: HarperSanFrancisco, 1992), 109.
5. C. S. Lewis, *The Horse and His Boy* (New York: Collier Books, 1970), 157–62.

CHAPTER 11

1. Frederick Buechner, *Listening to Your Life* (San Francisco: HarperSanFrancisco, 1992), 2.
2. Anne Morrow Lindbergh, *Gift from the Sea* (New York: Pantheon Books, 1955), 18.
3. Brother Lawrence, *The Practice of the Presence of God* (Uhrichsville, Ohio: Barbour Publishing, 1999), introduction.
4. Ibid., 37.
5. Ibid., 39.
6. Ibid., 45.
7. Frederick Buechner, *The Magnificent Defeat* (New York: Seabury Press, 1966), 44.
8. Kenneth Grahame, *The Wind in the Willows* (New York: Grosset & Dunlap, 1966), 115.
9. Ibid., 117
10. Ibid.
11. Ibid., 118.

CHAPTER 12

1. G. K. Chesterton, *Orthodoxy* (San Francisco: Ignatius Press, 1995), 151.
2. J. Keith Miller, "The Imprisonment and Release of the Soul: A Spiritual/Psychological Approach to Healing," a talk at the American Association of Christian Counselors Soul Care Conference, Nashville, Tennessee, 1999, audiotape.
3. J. Keith Miller, "Imprisonment and Release of the Soul," quoting from his book *The Secret Life of the Soul* (Nashville: Broadman and Holman, 1997).

An author and licensed professional counselor, Brenda Waggoner is passionate about helping women learn to live authentically with childlike joy and integrity in their relationships with God, with others, and with themselves. "As women, we have a myriad of life experiences, some pleasant and some painful," says Brenda. "We can become disillusioned in our faith and feel abandoned by God as we try to align our Christian beliefs with the realities we encounter."

A gifted storyteller, Brenda creatively weaves familiar themes of classic children's stories and fairy tales with dilemmas typical of a woman's everyday life, to offer encouragement and illustrate core biblical truths.

Brenda earned her bachelor's degree in counseling from Texas A&M University—Commerce and her master's degree in counseling from the University of North Texas. Her practice is currently affiliated with Bent Tree Counseling Center in Dallas. She works with women who struggle with anxiety, depression, and life transitions, and does play therapy with elementary-age children. "I'd been a Christian for more than twenty years," she says, "before I began to relate to God from my heart, believing that he really loved me, flaws and all." She believes her greatest therapeutic strengths are in the areas where she has personally struggled most.

Brenda and her husband, Frank, live in a hundred-year-old Victorian house in historic downtown McKinney, Texas, with their chocolate Labrador retriever, Molly. They enjoy taking walks in their nostalgic neighborhood, collecting and restoring old furniture, and having friends over for backyard or front-porch fun and food.

At age forty-one Brenda resumed the flute lessons she had given up as a teenager and spent two years playing with a "just for fun" woodwind quintet, sometimes entertaining small groups of women, children, or residents in nursing homes on special occasions. Today she enjoys playing flute and dancing as private forms of creative expression and worship. Between them, Brenda and Frank have three grown sons and a daughter-in-law, Scott, Jane, and Brent Whitson and Brandon Waggoner, all of whom live in Texas. They also have two "granddogs," Boomer and Gretzky.

If you are interested in having Brenda Waggoner speak at your women's retreat or workshop, please contact her office at (214) 757-4316, or visit her Web site, brendawaggoner.com.